THE THREE
OF LIFE

"I can't imagine how difficult it was to survive the circumstances experienced and it took a tremendous amount of courage to write about it. I would hope that this book provides guidance to other young women to help them avoid making bad decisions and knowing that it is never too late to turn their lives around."

~ UNCLE LENNY

First edition, 2012 Lisa Eva Gold
Copyright ©2012 Lisa Eva Gold Publshing
All rights reserved.

No part of this book may be reproduced, without permission from the publishers, unless by a reviewer who wishes to quote brief passages.

http//:www.thethreeoflifebook.yolasite.com

Manufactured in the USA

ISBN-10: 061555556X
EAN-13: 9780615555560

CONTENTS

Contents	*iii*
The Three of Life	*ix*
With Gratitude	*xiii*
Reflections	*xxix*
Authors Note	*xlv*
Preface	*xlvii*
Chapter One	1
Chapter Two	13
Chapter Three	25
Chapter Four	37
Chapter Five	47
Chapter Six	59
Chapter Seven	67
Chapter Eight	83
Chapter Nine	93
Chapter Ten	105
Epilogue	*111*
References	*115*

DOMESTIC VIOLENCE
(INTIMATE PARTNER VIOLENCE OR BATTERING)

- Domestic violence can be defined as a pattern of abusive behavior in any relationship that is used by one partner to gain or maintain power and control over an intimate partner.
- 1 in every 3 women will be victimized by domestic abuse.
- 1 in every 14 men will be physically assaulted by a current or former partner.
- In the United States, every nine seconds, a woman is abused by her boyfriend/partner. ~572,000 reports of domestic violence are reported on a yearly basis.
- 4.8 million women are a victim of an intimate partner-related physical assault and or rape every year. Sad but true, less than 20 percent of battered women seek medical treatment following an injury.
- 40% of domestic violence victims are males.
- The rate of intimate partner violence against females declined 53% between 1993 and 2008, from 9.4 victimizations per 1,000 females age 12 or older to 4.3 per 1,000. Against males, the rate declined 54%, from 1.8 victimizations per 1,000 males age 12 or older to 0.8 per 1,000.

Sexual Violence

- 232,960 crimes are *not* reported to the police by women in the U.S. alone. These statistics are based on reports of rape and or sexual assault which means more than 600 women every day experience assaults they do not report.

- A significant number of crimes are never even reported, usually because of the victim's feelings that nothing can or will be done about the personal nature of the incident.

Murder

- It is estimated that ten women a week are murdered in the U.S.; about one-third were killed by an intimate partner.

- Between 1993 and 2007 the overall rate of female homicides fell 43% from 4.18 to 2.38 homicides per 100,000 female U.S. residents.

- For more information log into

- www.OJP.USDOJ.GOV and/or http://www.ncvc.org/ncvc/Main.aspx

*Notes have been documented by Lisa Eva Gold from various meetings with various, Domestic Abuse and Human Trafficking committees. Reviews have also been noted through the National Crime Victimization and the Bureau of Justice Statistics.

"We don't report safe landings. If there is a crash and burn, we'll be there!"

~NATIONAL MEDIA

THE THREE OF LIFE

Attitude, Love and the Pursuit of Healthy Relationships

WRITTEN BY

LISA EVA GOLD

Visionary Life And Health Coach And Speaker

This book is dedicated to the countless Victims in our society.

*"Freedom Has A Voice;
May This Book Help You Find That Voice"*

WITH GRATITUDE

I am grateful for my many friends who have supported me in writing this book. especially thank those that have taken extra time with their supportive suggestions, comments and insights: Carol Peccarero, Jim Collins, Michelle Parker, my dearest friend, Debra and especially my Uncle Lenny. You have each read this book in its first draft phase, and I thank you. I am so blessed to have such great support.

I am also extremely grateful for my teenage daughter, Margo, who inspires me daily. By watching her grow and develop from childhood to adolescence, she teaches and shows me a healthy view of teenage years. I am so blessed to have this opportunity to be her Mother.

"The Three of Life, Attitude, Love and the Pursuit of Healthy Relationships", is a story that takes you on a personal and intimate journey that is based on true life occurrences. Names, phone numbers, and specific addresses have been changed to protect identities. In this book, confessions are reveled for the very first time. A closed door that has been blocked by shame and guilt is now open.

I hope this book may somehow help you heal as you also journey from Victim to Victory. I am not sure where this book will go, or how many copies will be sold or even how it will change you and your life. But I can tell you that in writing this book, old band-aids which have covered raw scars and wounds have been opened to breathe and heal by new perspectives and TLC (tender loving care).

We are forever growing and changing. Expecting to be wiser tomorrow than we are today and cherishing every experience and every person that comes into our lives to teach us something new. With faith in a higher power, believing in yourself and trusting your intuition, is your greatest teacher. However for some, trusting their intuition was not always their strength. For others, it took a lot of falling down and getting back up to find their own strength in honoring their intuition. God has created a masterpiece—YOU. Honor the gift of life.

I truly believe it is possible to live several lives in the existing body in which we are contained. It is a matter of positive attitudes, love and healthy relationships that we keep. It is not so much that the world changes around us but more so, it is our view that changes. More importantly it is what we change about ourselves.

I hope you enjoy this book and that it will give you greater insight into the importance of trusting in yourself and having confidence in yourself. Always keep in mind that trusting yourself and loving yourself first, makes the rest of the world and people in it easier to cope with.

I have learned that attitude is everything and love is what we are each made of. The importance of healthy relationships, lifts our spirits, strengthens our confidence and inspires love in life. To surround ourselves with people that lift us up, not tear us down, will only promote and increase our health and happiness.

With a will to move forward, each day lived is not the same. Each day brings with it new lessons and new experiences. It is important to keep in mind that we affect each new experience with our reactions, in attitude, in love and in the choices we make (partners, friends, careers, and possessions).

I would like to thank my church community at Christ Fellowship for their ongoing love and support. I would also like to bring attention to the many foster children that I mentor and work with. It has been an honor to work with each one of you. You have inspired me in ways that I cannot put into words. Seeing your strengths has made such a difference in my life.

And to my very dear family whom I cherish and love, as I grow older I realize what a gift it is to be in such a loving family. I am so grateful to be alive and well. To truly understand and know that attitude, love, and the pursuit for healthy relationships come from a divine power that flows through each and every one of us. Just by tapping into that God space of peace within and listening, you too can hear that still small voice that speaks the greatest truths.

You are only a victim if you allow yourself to be one.

⁂

The Abuse stops right here and right now.

⁂

Haven't you had enough?

DOMESTIC ABUSE

What is Domestic Abuse and are you a victim?

- Domestic abuse can be defined by an individual who is obsessive in power and control over a partner, spouse, child, employee or co-worker. The abuser is manipulative and controlling.

- There are no physical scars from psychological abuse as opposed to physical abuse; however, these psychological wounds are emotionally damaging and take longer to heal than physical scars.

- Identify whether you are being abused. Identify whether you are in danger. Save yourself and save your children. Make a decision to get out of the situation you are in. Call the National Domestic Abuse Hotline: #1-800—799—SAFE

DOMESTIC VIOLENCE IN FAMILIES

How does Domestic violence affect children?

- Studies suggest that 10 million children are affected by domestic violence and abuse in their home annually.

- Studies suggest that 3 out of 4 women have been sexually abused or assaulted in their lifetime.

- Studies suggest only 1 out of 5 women will report being abused, (rape, assault, etc).

Speak Your Truth

- If you are being abused, you may believe that you are to blame.

- If you are being abused, you may feel angry, sad, lonely, depressed and very confused. Don't feel helpless to stop the abuse.

- If you know of someone that is being abused, you can help just by listening, supporting and encouraging them to seek help.

DATING VIOLENCE

Is there such a thing as 'Dating Violence'?

- One in every five teens has experienced violence in a dating relationship.
- Abusive dating relationships occur with girls and women between the ages of 16 to 24. It is averaged that 1 out of every 5 adolescents is abused, and 1 out of every 4 women over the age of 24 is abused.
- Every 12 to 15 seconds there is an instance of domestic abuse.

FIND YOUR VOICE

- If the person you're involved with acts controlling, aggressive, coercive or violent, that is abuse!
- Relationships can be abusive even if there is no hitting. Abuse can be verbal, emotional, physical or sexual or even a combination of these.
- Trust your instincts. If you are in immediate danger, get help by dialing 911. Follow through by seeking counseling with victim services. Call your local church for guidance. Call the operator to connect you with the local crisis hotline.

VICTIMIZED

Having borne the burden of the cross I have carried; faith has been my rock. Can you relate?

- **SHATTERED** — But not broken.
- **WOUNDED** — But healed with time.
- **DEVISTATED** — Yet with faith and devotion I have been refined.

Freedom Comes From Within, Not Woithout

- History repeats itself; the only way to change history is to not repeat it.
- Choose to break the cycle of being victimized.
- Turn your negative experiences into positive by helping others in your community to overcome and repair damages that have been done because of abuse.

A PURPOSE IN LIFE

Do your intentions define your purpose?

- 🥀 Think about your intentions for this day.
- 🥀 Understand that intentions are created with purpose.
- 🥀 Your intentions will have an effect others.

You Are In Control Of You

- 🥀 It is only healthy to align our **A**ctions with purpose. Everything we do comes from a place of **L**ove, as this is the greatest power on earth.
- 🥀 **I**ntegrity is the essence of everything; being **G**ood and **N**oble is linked to a healthy **M**indset, as you are what you think you are.
- 🥀 **E**nrichment comes from helping others live a better life, linked to being conscious in **N**oticing our very own **T**arget of intentions, as you must be rationally in **A.L.I.G.N.M.E.N.T.** with your highest power.

Your journey has molded you for your greater good, and it was exactly what it needed to be. Don't think that you've lost time. There is no short-cutting to life. It took each and every situation you have encountered to bring you to the now. And now is right on time.

—ASHA TYSON

REFLECTIONS

In my last book, "A Will to Survive", I share a chapter of my life that reflects on how trying to balance a career, a family life and an irreconcilable marriage falls apart, after I had been misdiagnosed with Chronic Fatigue. A misdiagnosis that was a blessing in disguise as it enabled me to re-evaluate my life choices. In "A Will to Survive", I promised my readers that I would fill in the missing pieces in this book that you now hold in your hands. However, after careful consideration, "A Will to Survive" is a book based on a toxic relationship/marriage and the basis of the story has already been told.

The Three of Life is a book that is focused on someone else's story.

Over the years, I have dedicated a lot of my time in mentoring foster children. They have each brought such a gift to my life. A gift that has allowed me to mentally take a few steps back and truly re-evaluate the true meaning of relationships. Each child I have worked with, has a tragic story to tell of being lost and misguided without direction. The only way that they are able to see through these tragedies, is with the support of mentors and teachers whom inspire them to grow stronger in supporting them and believing in them.

In writing this story, my purpose is to reach out to you, the reader and inspire you to think about your choices, whom you include and how you create your own destiny.

My story focuses on a young woman named Jinni Erica Montgomery. I met Jinni when she was only Eighteen years old. She was aging out of the foster care system at the time and I promised to keep in touch with her. Over the years, her experiences for seeking approval have disappointed me. Yet, she has continued to inspire me with her unyielding attitude and charm with a love for life, like no other.

Jinni is an attractive white girl with long blond straight hair and green eyes. Jinni has a mystical look about her that seems to be intriguing to everyone that meets her. What I see is a young woman, that thrives on living for acceptance and approval, yet her unyielding attitude and charm tell me that she is more than just a pretty face.

Jinni grew up very confused as her motives were not clearly defined or focused. Her influences were confusing as feeling powerless became second nature. It seemed as though the words, 'clear intentions' did not exist in her dictionary. Jinni's perception of reality had been clouded, yet all along she had a deeper yearning to seek the truth and beauty that life truly offers.

Although Jinni comes from a middle class family, she lacked guidance and support as her families priority was focused on entertaining, and throwing big parties with friends. Details about Jinni's family are not what is important in this story. Jinni's name has been changed to protect her identity. As I have promised, her story would help others with out her having to disclose her identity.

In opening up and sharing her story, she has opened a closed door of her past that has only held her back. As misguidance only sent her seeking acceptance in all the wrong places and attracting all the wrong people. Jinni struggles over so many years seeking to find that one stable relationship. Her story will touch readers as she thrives for stability, clarity and peace. Maybe that is what we all long for? Yet, in search of these treasures buried within each one of us, it is so easy to get lost without.

So many women grow up, feeling neglected and unsupported. Somewhere along their Journey in life, bad choices are created out of uncertainty and misunderstandings. Traveling on a road with no directions is a feeling, like being dust in the wind. A life's journey does not feel like a success, rather it feels unclear as years gone by seemed to have been lost.

I recall growing up; my Dad had always said to me, "Lisa, life is like a smorgasbord. You have to try a little of everything before you know what you really like." The only problem with that advice was that I found I liked a variety. With a variety, and without a focus, it had been a very difficult road to walk for me.

I have learned that having no focus and not knowing who we truly are smothers the soul and stunts our growth. With our energy scattered about, we tend to attract people of all sorts, and many of those people do not serve our higher purpose. Without focus, we lose sight of not only who we are, but more importantly, what we want and where we are going in life. We lose sight of that light at the end of the tunnel.

Without focus, we make poor decisions because we are blinded to see clearly the best choice. So many times as we travel on our journey we truly feel alone; we get discouraged and feel that no one cares about us. We feel that there is never anyone there to support us; yet, the reality is we have not been there to support ourselves. Therefore we go about life blaming our family and friends for neglecting us when we are truly the ones to blame because we have neglected ourselves !

How could we expect someone else to support our missions when we are scattered and uncertain ourselves? Believe it or not, YOU are your greatest teacher; I am MY greatest teacher. Knowing your guided intention behind the choices you make has a significant effect on what the outcome may be. Focus on your destination and have faith in getting there. It's not always the 'how' we get to where we are going, but more importantly it's the attitude we keep on our journey in getting there that makes a difference.

Recognize the relationships you have on this journey and realize who is there to support you in your missions. Most importantly, realize that YOUR choices are going to affect someone else. It is important to be mindful of your attitude and be aware of whom will be effected by your choices, directly or indirectly.

Through various letters, and many more phone calls, Jinni, has inspired me to create **The Three of Life**. As her actions spoke in one way, I understood her in another way. As it became clear to me that refining her *attitude*, loving herself more and realizing that between *love* and *healthy relationships*, life does not have much more meaning than these three; **Attitude, Love, Healthy Relationships**.

You and I are essentially infinite choice-makers. In every moment of our existence, we are in that field of all possibilities where we have access to an infinity of choices.
~ DEEPAK CHOPRA

THE CHILD WITHIN

Walked through an art museum filled with pictures of style and color.
Came upon a portrait that was like no other.
Portrait of a young girl, hair pulled back wearing a dress of blue;
she held a lit candle standing alone in the dark.
Wondered who she was and why I looked back.

Saw the reflection and continued to stare back.
It's the child inside of me that cried out;
She's been hidden for so long
I believe she'd forgotten her own song.

Because of the guilt, because of the shame, I told her to go away.
From past to present, she has always been.
It's life's lessons that have created the grown up she is.
I'd forgotten all about her............until today.

It's the child inside.
It is clear to see that child inside is me.
She'd grown used to the dark,
Let her eyes adjust.
As she blows out the candle and walks into the sunrise,
Give her some time to realign
For it is I, the child inside.

~2008(c) Lisa Eva Gold

"We've learned to lay our failures and problems conveniently at the feet of others. "I can't do anything about the way I am," a seriously troubled man said to me. "My childhood was a nightmare." Twenty years later this man's life was still on hold because of unhealed wounds. It has become apparent that the heart of his problem was not so much his troublesome past, but his compulsion to dwell on it without doing anything about it. Depression, neurosis, chronic unhappiness is not only caused by an event of a person, but also how a person continues to respond to them. When we realize that we are responsible for freeing ourselves from yokes of the past, we will also free everyone else of this responsibility. Only then can we begin to concentrate more on loving and less on blaming".

~ LEO BUSCAGLIA

August 2, 2009

I stand here numb. The reality of my dad's passing has not settled with me yet. This tragedy seems like a bad dream, as I stand before my father's grave.

How can I begin to tell you about my dad?

There is so much to say. I am not sure where to begin..........

My dad was a character in his own right. He had different sides to him; as a parent he was strict, yet I remember him being goofy and silly. However, when he would catch himself being silly or goofy he would immediately take a 180 degree turn and get very serious. As a kid, this behavior made having a sense of humor a little confusing.

I remember one year after trick or treating, my dad would go through my candy bag and pull out all the candy that he liked. Of course, I did not like the fact that Dad was eating my candy, so every year after that, I hid my candy bag so that Dad would not eat my candy.

I remember being seven years old when I went to see my first movie with Dad. He loved going to the movies and the very first movie he took me to see was a Chuck Norris movie. Prior to seeing the film, I recall Dad saying, "Lisa I am taking you to see this film so you will know what the real world is like." I cannot say I agree with that philosophy, but Dad took me to see many other films that I probably would not take my twelve year old daughter to see today. Nevertheless, my father loved going to the movies.

I recall traveling many places around the world with Dad and my family growing up. I especially remember the father/daughter trip to Greece we took. That had to have been the best trip ever. I had a great time seeing all the sites and the artifacts.

I remember I had taken the book, "The Amityville Horror" with me. It was night time and I was going to sleep, and Dad asked me what I had been reading. I told him and he said, "Let me take a look at that." So, I handed him the book and went to sleep. The next morning, Dad said angrily, "Lisa, we need to have talk! It's all your fault!" I trembled with fear thinking I had done something wrong, when he turned to me with a smile on his face and a chuckle in his speech and said, "You shouldn't have given me that book! I did not sleep all night. It was so good, I couldn't put it down and so I stayed up all night and finished it".

As an adult living in a different state, I talked to my dad every day, sometimes three times a day. I recall many times he would call me and I would roll my eyes and think, "It's Dad again, what more could I possibly talk about with him today?" Every day, Dad would call, and the first thing he would say to me was, "So what's new?" And I would think, "Geez, I just spoke with you yesterday Dad!" Yet, for Dad, every day was a new day; a new beginning and a new adventure. And I found that I did have something new to share with him every day.

As time went on and I got used to his phone calls, I found comfort in our conversations. My dad was my closest confidant, and at times my biggest headache. He was my friend at times and other times he would forget my age and feel the need to scold me. My dad was funny like that. He was an amazing person. He was invincible it seemed to me. He made me nervous most of the time because of the amount of energy he had. He loved life and always wanted to learn more. Dad loved to travel and be everywhere and anywhere he was able to go. He loved the adventure that life offered and meeting new people, and he never forgot anyone he meet. Years could pass and Dad would always say, "Remember so and so? What ever happened to them?"

Dad loved his family and he loved his work with airplanes. He was resilient; He believed in himself and honored himself the way we all should by following our dreams and not letting anyone get in our way of our own will.

Dad was my inspiration. It seems as though I have had many struggles throughout my own life. My life has not been easy; yet, Dad was always there for me to guide me and to console me with soothing conversation. It seems as though the past three years or so, I have found my own path and am truly happy with my life and my accomplishments. The week before my Dad passed he said to me, "Lisa I am so very proud of you." It seems as though I had waited all my life to hear those words from him. And I knew he meant what he said. I am happy that I made my Dad proud of me.

May you rest in peace Dad, and when your soul is settled, may you soar like the eagle you are, for you always were a free spirit.

Love you Dad..........

JAPAN 2008

"Hope these photos came out ok. Had some time today and went to the city and went to the Imperial Palace. A lot of changes have been made here since last being here. The old seems to disappear as the new comes in. The building does not seem to stop and it is becoming like New York. Too many people and the dress and customs seemed to have disappeared. The grounds of the Imperial Palace are well kept and it still stands strong since the late 1500 hundreds. You will note that a few of the trees (Cherry Blossoms) are starting to bloom a little early as the weather is still cold. I guess I miss the old customs of Japan and I hate to see it go." ~**JACK GOLD**

(Dad sent me an email that included 35 pictures. This was one of my favorite pictures received February 10th, 2008).

XL   THE THREE OF LIFE

JAPAN 2008

Cherry Tree In Blossom

When I was an infant, Dad, a man of many talents, painted an oil replica of Napoleon Bonaparte crossing the Alps (after having taken power in France during the 18 Brumaire on November 9, 1799). The original painting is by the French artist Jacques-Louis David (painted between 1801 and 1805).

I never really understood why this picture was hung in my home. In fact, in all honesty, I thought the picture was a bit tacky. I always wondered how or why it was a portrait of influence for my father.

A BRIEF HISTORY OF NAPOLEON BONAPARTE

Born into a Christian family, Napoleon was shy, proud, willful, unkempt and untrained as a child. He was little, pale, and nervous and almost without instruction. Yet already enamored by a soldier's life and conscious of a certain sense of superiority over his peers, he was suddenly transplanted from his free life to an environment foreign in its language, artificial in its etiquette, and severe in its regulations. Young Bonaparte learned to hate the idea of oppression and was a boy contemptuous of necessity. He even despised his father's submission and his mother's lack of time for her children's training. His father gave them no attention and labeled Napoleon as an "obstinate and curious child." He was the second of eight children. He was domineering over his brothers and companions, fearing no one. He ran wild on the beach with the sailors or over the mountains with the herdsmen listening to their tales of the Corsican rebellion and of fights, on sea and land, imbibing their contempt for submission and their love for liberty. As an adult, Napoleon served as a second lieutenant in La Fère artillery regiment. After the outbreak of the French Revolution, Napoleon was determined to return to Italy to reinforce the French troops in the country and retake the territory seized by the Austrians in the preceding years. In the spring of 1800, he led the Reserve Army across the Alps through the Great St. Bernard Pass. The Austrian forces, under Michael von Melas, lay siege to Masséna in Genoa, and Napoleon hoped to gain the element of surprise by taking the trans – Alpine route. By the time Napoleon's troops arrived, Genoa had fallen. But he pushed ahead, hoping to engage the Austrians before they could regroup. The Reserve Army fought a battle at Montebello on June 9th, before eventually securing a decisive victory at the Battle of Marengo. Now, as First Consul and with the French victory in Italy, it allowed for a rapprochement with Charles IV of Spain. While talks were underway to re establish diplomatic relations, a traditional exchange of gifts took place. Charles received Versailles-manufactured pistols, dresses from the best Parisian dressmakers, jewels for the queen, and a fine set of armor for the newly reappointed Prime Minister, Manuel Godoy. In return, Napoleon was offered sixteen Spanish horses from the royal stables, portraits of the king and queen by Goya and a portrait of Napoleon himself, that was to be commissioned from David. The French ambassador to Spain, Charles-Jean-Marie Alquier, requested the original painting from David on Charles' behalf. The portrait was to hang in the Royal Palace of Madrid as a token of the new relationship between the two countries. David, who had been an ardent supporter of the Revolution but had transferred his fervor to the new Consulate, was eager to undertake the commission. On learning of the request, Bonaparte instructed David to produce three further versions: one for the Château de Saint – Cloud, one for the library of Les Invalides and a third for the palace of the Cisalpine Republic in Milan. A fifth version was produced by David and remained in his workshops until his death. [Researched through; www.Wikipedia.org]

Now, looking back and knowing a bit of history behind this painting; I understand why Napoleon was such an influence for my dad.

Dad was a leader who conquered every challenge in his life, not letting anyone get in his way. He was a rebel in his own time. My dad's childhood years had been filled with rejection, grief, neglect and parental alcoholism. His mom died when he was very young, and his dad was an alcoholic that never paid attention to him. My grandfather placed my dad and his brother and sister in foster care at a very young age. Later, my grandfather retrieved my dad, his brother and sister when he was able to find a new wife and gain some sobriety in his life. Possibly my dad admired Napoleon because he could relate to his proud, noble and resilient character.

I believe I will never meet anyone like my dad. He thrived on the adventure of life. Every day was a new day for Dad. His greatest love was his work. As an airplane pilot, his perseverance and ambition to travel and meet people of all cultures gave him so many stories told and untold. I wonder if he ever thought about what a legacy he would leave. He truly was one of a kind. As for the picture of Napoleon Bonaparte, it is sketched in my memory bank. Maybe the picture was hung to portray:

"Proud and Noble; Fear not and conquer all that blocks your path."

~Lisa Eva Gold

AUTHOR'S NOTE

After my Dads passing, I realized how hard my father tried to be an impressionist. He never forgot any of his experiences, as he always had a story to tell of the past. He held on to his pains and never let himself or anyone forget. Maybe that's why my Dad never sat still long enough to smell the roses. He was always so busy doing something creative, to keep his mind occupied.

Seeing how proud my Dad always was despite his challenges, has taught me that to move on in life we must free ourselves of our past pains despite how hard they were. In order to do so we must look at what we have learned and turn those negative experiences inside out and use them as a teacher rather than dwell in a doubtful existence.

For many of us we find that trusting in a higher power, in a God is the only way. For some of us, it takes a lot of pain, a lot of grief and a lot of darkness, before we are able to know what it means to surrender ourselves to our higher power. "THE THREE of LIFE, Attitude, Love and the Pursuit of Healthy Relationships", is a book focused on healing pain and finding your voice to say that you know better now. My hope is that this book will help you look at your life from a different perspective. Please remember that the experiences you have had, are lessons that have taught you to be the better person that you are today.

Please know that you are not alone in your journey of life. You are loved more than you know. If you find yourself in a stuck place, find your voice and speak your truth! Speak up for you because you are special and there is no one else like YOU!

You cannot transcend what you do not know. To go beyond Yourself you must know yourself.

—SRI NISARGADATTA MAHARAJ

PREFACE

Everything written in this book is based on a motivation to survive; an internal drive to move forward. There is no appointment and no prescription to its remedy. The overall intention for writing this book is to bring you closer to your true purpose in life and to fill you with hope for tomorrow:

- Hope to make better choices in your life. ~Hope for you to find your voice. ~Hope for you to speak up and truly believe how important you really are. ~Hope for you to see each day as a gift. It is only you who are responsible for the choices you make. ~Hope for you to know that it's ok to honor yourself. You do not owe anyone an explanation for what you think or how you feel. You are entitled to be all that you are.
- Be encouraged to make each day a great day!
- You are in control of you!

You owe it to yourself to BE everything you truly are. Like a tree with many branches, so it is with you and me. Do not be afraid to grow, to learn, and to do everything you ever dreamed of.

- Take time to know who you are. Only you can find that treasure within!

"By banishing doubt and trusting your intuitive feelings, you clear a space for the power of intention to flow through."

~ DR. DWAYNE DYER

"We have to serve our self many years before we gain our own confidence."

~HENRY S HASKINS 1878-1957

THE THREE OF LIFE

1. Attitude
2. Love
3. Healthy Relationships

Dear Jinni~

It is said that when a caterpillar has transformed into a butterfly; that same butterfly will continue to revisit that same branch of a tree on which it made its transformation.

    Until that butterfly feels safe and complete on that branch of a tree, then is when it is time for that butterfly to visit other branches.

    So it is with each of our life lessons.

With much Love ~*Ms. Lisa*

Nightmares of Reality

Dearest Ms. Lisa,

I realize it's been at least a year or so since we spoke, but I am dealing with lot and I am not really sure who else to turn too. I will just have to fill you in on what my life has been like. I am hoping you can maybe help me. You always say the right things and seem to really care. I suppose I should start by telling you that I moved to a small town in Connecticut. So I could attend a preppy two-year private school. I moved into the girl's dormitory house that overlooked the Thames River. The view from my window was beautiful.

I majored in Psychology with a minor in Education. I had thought I might like to be a psychologist or maybe a teacher. Underlying the reality of my choice in majors, there was a real need for me to understand myself; make sense of my life, especially my childhood.

I recall I got along well with my teachers/professors, and it was important to me that I follow through on projects and try to get good grades. I had a lot of fun in college. Probably more fun than I should have. I partied a lot and hung out when I should have been studying. I had maybe a 2.8 GPA, not a very good GPA, yet I would convince myself that it was close to a 3.0 GPA which wasn't too bad.

During this first year of college, when I was home on breaks, I had a job as a cashier at a local delicatessen. It was fun and the people I worked with were nice. It was just a summer kind of job. No major memories here other than the band Jethro Tull, which was a popular subject.

After attending college for one year in Connecticut, I wanted to move back to New York to attend school. I had applied and gotten accepted for a transfer to a prestigious University in New York. This time, I was an Education major with a minor in Psychology (the idea of becoming a teacher and having summer vacations was very inviting). I moved on to campus and just loved being on a bigger campus that had three times the number of students, than the previous school in Connecticut. I partied just as much, if not more!

In all honesty, my grades got worse. I can recall this one class, Philosophy. I had a term paper to write, yet I did not bother reading the material required. It was very time consuming, and I wanted to hang out and have fun. So, for this term paper, I read the brief subject material theme and just improvised. I remember my philosophy teacher scheduled a meeting with me one afternoon after I handed in my paper.

We sat on a bench outside the classroom and he told me that my paper was just great! He was very kind and gentle in his approach. The only problem, he said, was that my paper did not have anything to do with the topic theme;

therefore, he could not give me a passing grade. My other class grades were not improving and I questioned my integrity. After the first semester, I dropped out of school.

As you know my parents had been divorced almost two years by now. I had lived with my mom, my Grandmother, my Aunt and in the foster home on and off throughout high school and visited with my dad whenever he was available. After college, I moved back home with my mother. She was dating and having a lot of fun with her new-found freedom. In all honesty, it was kind of scary at age eighteen to watch my mother act like she was eighteen too.

I recall that Mom owned her own hair salon, MAGNIFICO, in our hometown. She had asked me to work for her when I wasn't attending school. She asked me to be her secretary. Just food for thought here, I would not have hired me. I was late to work all the time and I had a poor attitude when helping my Mother. Nevertheless, I continued to help her.

There was a delicatessen that was next door to Mom's hair salon. One day Mom told me that the guy that worked there liked me. She told me that he asked her if it was ok to ask me out, and she thought it was a good idea. She said that he was a nice guy. I was amused and flattered by this. So I expected him to ask me out the next time I went in to order lunch.

He was a tall, average looking guy with long blond hair. His name was "Mooky" (no, this is not a typo). Mooky did ask me to go out that coming Friday night, and I agreed without hesitation.

We went out to dinner and then back to Mooky's house to meet his parents. They lived in a very nice home and both his parents were very nice. The only downfall to this night was that I was really not attracted to Mooky and I did not like him the way he liked me.

We dated a couple of times. I felt like I was kissing my brother when we kissed. (That's as far as that went.). On the second date, we went to a local bar, local to his hometown in the suburbs of, New York. There he met up with some of his friends whom I had not met before. I was immediately attracted to one of his friends, Jeremy. Jeremy was a sharp looking guy who dressed well.

Within the next week or so, Jeremy and I were dating. Jeremy and I spoke to Mooky about Jeremy and I now being a couple. Mooky had been heartbroken and I kind of felt sad because Mooky was genuinely a good guy, even if his friends always talked down about him.

I thought this guy Jeremy was the cat's meow. He drove a big truck and he worked as a mechanic. I can recall his big, metallic blue truck with tire flaps which had flap girl decals. I was smitten by a mechanic with flap girl decals on his truck. I suppose in all honesty, I would not look at what a person does for work to define them (and so it has been). Yet, seriously, sometimes I really worry about me. Did I watch too many episodes of, "Dukes of Hazards" growing up? Was I scarred in some way? I truly questioned my integrity here.

Well, on with my story. Jeremy and I were dating. I thought at first that Jeremy was funny as he frequently imitated Jack Nicholson's character from the movie, 'The Shining.' I thought it was funny until much later on in our relationship, when that character really came to life.

I got to meet Jeremy's parents who lived in a nice neighborhood near Mooky. Jeremy had one sister, Claudine. She did not live at home full-time. She was severely mentally and physically challenged; therefore, Jeremy's parents had placed her in a home that would be able to take better care of her needs. Yet she would still visit home on occasion via a handicap transportation van.

I don't remember specific dates or the chronology of this time in my life. So I am just going to tell you what I remember-

Jeremy liked to drink alcohol frequently. He was an abusive drunk. I drank socially, but alcohol put me to sleep. We frequently visited this local pub on the weekends, as it was a familiar place.

After hanging out at the local pub, there were times when Jeremy and I would return to or what I did, but he would hit me. Not only would he hit me, he would wrestle me to the ground outside of his house on the lawn. He would yell at the top of his lungs and call me every curse word you can think of. It wasn't long before most of the neighbors would be standing outside their front doors in their pajamas, watching to see what the noise was all about. Why didn't anyone help me? Why couldn't I help myself and walk out of this nightmare of a relationship? Did I believe, at the time, that I was not good enough to be treated with respect and dignity? Maybe, I was the one who did not respect me to begin with?

On these nightly events, eventually, after I was thrown around and beat up long enough, Jeremy's parents would come outside. They would pull Jeremy off me. They wouldn't ask questions and did not think much of the situation. Usually they would just invite me in to sleep in the basement on the sofa couch. I felt so uncomfortable staying at their house. Jeremy's Mom was a perfectionist and her house was as clean as a hospital. Our relationship was not stable and I did not feel safe.

One time, Jeremy and I were invited to his parent's house for dinner. Jeremy told me that we needed to keep an eye on the time and that we shouldn't be late because it would upset his mom. The first time we were invited for dinner, we were five minutes late.

We walked in his parent's house, and his mom began a dramatic episode by screaming at the top of her lungs letting us know that we are late. We walked upstairs to where the kitchen was and she was yelling, "Where were you? YOU are BOTH late!!!!" With that she picked up a full bottle of ketchup that was on the counter in front of her and threw it at me. I quickly swerved out of the way as the ketchup bottle just swiped my head and slammed into the wall behind me. Not only did this make a hole in the wall, but ketchup splattered everywhere on the wall and all over me. I was terrified and in shock as she stood there and laughed.

I was paralyzed with fear. I did not know how to react. After she finished laughing, she told me to go take a shower in the bathroom and wash my hair. Her house was obsessively immaculate, and I was honestly afraid to even use the bathroom. She told me to hurry up because dinner was cold. I quickly washed up and wrapped my hair in a towel. I returned to the kitchen where Jeremy, his mom and his dad were sitting at the table eating. I sat down and Jeremy's mom stared at me and laughed again. She told me that I looked like Aunt Jemima.

Why couldn't I help myself? Why did I stay in this relationship? I was so very afraid of everything about this relationship, yet, what kept me in it?

After this incident, I was numb. I continued to date Jeremy. (Why, I don't know). Sometimes he would come to my mom's house, yet most of the time, I would go to his house. I recall each time I would ring the doorbell I would hear Jeremy's mother from the basement television room yell, "Is that her again? I would stand outside and my stomach would tremble.

The holidays came and went and shortly after Christmas time, I went over to Jeremy's parent's house. I could hear his mother's voice yet again in that wretched tone, "Is that her again?!" In response I said, "Hi, Mrs. Moreau." She responded with; "Jinni, I was cleaning the den this morning and I found a strand of your hair!" How does one respond to this? My stomach turned and I felt terribly uncomfortable.

After Jeremy and I had been dating a few months, my mom's business was not doing well, and she had to close her shop. In the meantime, I really wanted to move out of my mom's house and have my own space in my own apartment. As my mom continued to work for herself as a hairdresser, she moved her business back into the cellar of our house Upstate, New York, to the shop my Dad had previously built for her when they were still married.

In the meantime, I found an apartment that was listed in the newspaper. The listing was for a remodeled studio apartment in the Bronx. I called and scheduled a time to see the apartment. When I arrived at the house, I rang the doorbell. Soon the door opened and there stood an average looking business man dressed in business slacks and a button down, formal collared shirt. He was approximately 5'6" in height, had brown eyes, and wore his brown hair slicked back. He looked to be in his early to mid-thirties. His name was Reed. I interviewed with Reed to rent the apartment from him. I kind of felt uneasy about Reed, but I was uneasy about all the relationships in my life.

Reed took me around the back of the house where the apartment was. We walked down five steps and entered in through a basement door. Walking into the studio, I could see directly in front of me a very nice, new, small kitchen, with a closed door facing the entrance door which was the bathroom. To the right of me was a cubical sized space and a double door closet. I was surprised to open these doors up to find that it was the boiler room. The third closed door, to the left of the entrance way, was a very small closet that had a piece of plywood, barricading what looked like another room. The plywood stood maybe four footsteps into the closet. Reed had told me that another lady rented/lived on the opposite side of this plywood barricade. I was really uncomfortable about this. Yet, as usual, I did not pay any attention to how I felt. I agreed to rent the apartment for four hundred dollars a month. I gave him first and last month's security deposit. The next weekend, my mom helped me move into my studio apartment.

I was eighteen years old and was so very excited to be in my first apartment. I moved in on a Friday and it took us most of the afternoon. We moved my Futon bed, a small dresser/ book shelf, a television and television stand, and several boxes and groceries. My mom left once we moved everything in. She offered to stay and help me unpack. I thanked her but told her I wanted to unpack myself. It was such an exciting time for me and I felt so grown up.

My mom wished me well and told me she would call me later or tomorrow. I spent several hours unpacking, decorating, and getting myself organized. My phone rang late in the afternoon and it was my landlord, Reed. He told me to come upstairs around seven in the evening. He told me that I needed to sign some more papers that he forgot to give me. He also wanted to discuss a few rules about the property. I honestly did not think anything of this, and before I knew it, seven o'clock arrived. I left my apartment and walked around the house to the front door. The screen door was closed, but the front door was open. I did not even bother to ring the bell; I just said "Hello?" and Reed immediately came to greet me. He was very formal and appeared to be very cordial as he opened the screen door for me and welcomed me in, he smiled and closed the front door and locked it.

My stomach knotted up and I felt very vulnerable. Reed invited me to sit down and he offered me a drink. I declined, as I was exhausted, and I was just really looking forward to getting back downstairs to relax and watch some television. I told him I had been busy all day moving in and unpacking. He was very charming and verbalized to me how and verbalized to me how pleased he was to have me as his tenant. I was beginning to think that there really weren't any other papers to sign.

"Let me show you around my place," Reed insisted. As I began to feel uneasy, my stomach tied in knots. Trying to stay polite I said, "Ok." He pointed out the very obvious living room where the front door entered into the room where we had been standing. Then to the left of the living room area, he took me into a large kitchen area and behind the kitchen there were four closed doors. He told me that he could not show me all the rooms because there were two other girls that rented from him as well. Each had her own bedroom. The third door was the bathroom, and then he took my hand and pulled me into his bedroom, the fourth room, shut the door and locked it. He began making physical advancements as he continued to be very charming with sweet talking words. I tried to figure out how to get myself out of this situation. I told him I was all sweaty from moving all day and I really was not in any shape to be fooling around with anyone.

He told me it did not matter. All I could think about was going back downstairs to my apartment. He began to take my clothes off, and I was just so afraid to do anything. We lay in his bed, and as we had sex, he told me all the nice things guys say. Yet, my stomach felt all knotted up, and my mind kept saying, "I just want to go home." I had this terrible feeling about everything that was going on. Yet, I could not make sense of it. When we were finished, he asked me to sleep In his bed and stay the night. I told him that I really needed to get back downstairs. He seemed angry, and I was afraid he would not let me leave.

When I got back downstairs, I felt so disgusting and so very violated that I immediately went into my bathroom, sobbing, and grabbed the douche I had placed under my sink earlier when unpacking my toiletries. I needed to clean myself because I felt so dirty. When I came out of the bathroom still crying, I could see the bottle of Champaign my mom had bought me to drink with my friends to celebrate my first apartment. I opened the bottle, turned on the television, and drank straight from the bottle until I passed out. When I awoke in the morning, I found myself lying face-down on my futon, with the television still on, and the empty Champaign bottle sitting on the floor in front of where I had fallen asleep.

My phone rang and it was my boyfriend, Jeremy. He interrogated me and wondered why I did not answer the phone last night when he called. I said I had been busy unpacking all day and passed out, not hearing the telephone. He told me he had to work even though it was a Saturday, but that he would come over to see my new apartment later Saturday evening. I believe I just ran errands that day; I was still buying new decor for my apartment. It was like any other day, except that I walked around, with a lump in my throat and a cringing stomach ache. I was just emotionally numb.

I had spoken to some of my girlfriends, and they agreed to pass by and visit when they could. They agreed to call me when they would be in the area. That evening, Jeremy had visited, and I cooked my first meal on the gas stove and made a tossed salad on the side. It was fun to be in my own place, so it seemed. I had a new job, which I would be starting that coming Monday, as a data entry sales technician at a local company close to the place where Jeremy lived with his parents.

My job required me to be on the phone for eight hours taking information for sales products. The people were very nice and the job seemed easy. It was not a cold calling job; it was a job where people called in to place orders. I don't even remember what I was selling, I only remember I had the job for a few months and I liked working there.

So there I was in my new apartment with a new job to look forward to as well. My dad called me and wanted to visit me in my new place. I was so excited and nervous to have him visit. I wondered what he would think of my new place. My parents had been divorced and I did not talk to my Dad as much as I did with my mom. Soon, Dad came to visit and it felt strange for me to be serving him snacks and a cold drink of soda. He seemed to like my place and wished me lots of luck. He told me if I needed anything that he was there for me. Knowing my dad and how judgmental he could be, I just smiled.

Mid-week I received a call from my landlord. He told me that he was having a party at his house next Saturday night to watch the heavy weight, Hulk Hogan, wrestle. He invited me to go and I told him I wasn't sure if I could, but I would try my best to be there. I hung up the phone and my stomach felt like cement. In the meantime, my private parts, had been feeling very uncomfortable. I went to the party Saturday night and Reed greeted me with an evil eye and introduced me to his friends. I felt really out of place. Even more uncomfortable because Reed kept looking at me in a strange way, and each time he did, my stomach turned.

I had seen Jeremy Friday and lied to him about having plans with my girlfriends Saturday night. Friday we had gone to hang out to the local pub. And as usual he got crazy drunk getting physically and verbally abusive, calling me bitch and grabbing me by my hair and pulling and pushing me around for his amusement. It was not anything I was not already used too. On Sunday, we visited with his parents (how I hated visiting with them).

That night at my apartment, I reminded myself that I made it through my very first full week in my very own apartment. I was very excited but at the same time denying all the relationships in my life.

Monday morning arrived and it was time to get up and get ready to go to work. When I had gotten up to take a shower and get ready for work, I noticed these lumps on my private area. It looked like I had chicken pox again. I had chicken pox when I was a kid, and that was not fun. Later that day, I called my gynecologist's office to schedule an appointment for later in the week.

Work was a day full of training and learning the sales pitch. I was exhausted when I got home. The next day when I awoke, I noticed that not only did I have chicken pox bumps, but I also had hives all over my vagina. Needless to say, I was beside myself. I was so disgusted with myself; I just hated myself.

When I spoke to my boyfriend Jeremy, I told him that I needed to talk to him in person about some private issues. We made arrangements to meet after work that Wednesday. Instead of me telling him what happened with my landlord, I accusingly asked him if he had a girlfriend. He denied having one. Yet I blamed him that I had these breakouts on my genitals and that I needed to go to the doctor. Worse yet, I told him it was his fault. He did not comment.

I had all these emotions going on inside of me. I did not know how to act or who to turn to. I was so angry with myself for being in this abusive relationship with Jeremy and I was even angrier at myself for being raped by my landlord. I was so afraid of what Jeremy would do to me if I told him what happened with my landlord. So I buried the truth and turned it into blame. Blame and shame on me and blame on my boyfriend. That Friday, I had Jeremy drive me to the gynecologist's office.

After my exam, the Doctor told me that I had an STD. "Oh great!" I thought. Just more reasons to hate ME. All I could think about was how disgusting I felt. I could not comprehend any of this. The doctor's office set me up for six weeks of treatments.

Each treatment at the gynecologist's office was an unforgettable experience. The doctor would use a Freezer gun to burn off what looked like chicken pox off my vagina. He told me that this STD virus (the name I cannot even pronounce), is curable through this series of treatments. A miserable six weeks of treatments was a nightmare. I truly hated myself; I hated my life; I hated ME! It was my entire fault.

> "O innocent **victims** of Cupid,
> Remember this little verse:
> To let a fool kiss you is stupid,
> To let a kiss fool you is worse."

~E.Y Hayrberg

THE THREE OF LIFE
reminds me to think about;

ATTITUDE = Ignorance comes from fear.

LOVE = It is hard to love yourself when your self image is damaged.

HEALTHY RELATIONSHIPS = Are not possible when we are not Grounded and in alignment with ourselves first.

"*It is hard enough to deal with other people's judgments placed upon you, but it is even harder and more destructive to deal with judgments you have placed upon yourself.*"

~Unknown

Broken Boundaries

It had been a very long and difficult six weeks. I was still working nine to five, Monday through Friday. It was shortly after the six weeks of medical treatments that I got a call from my Uncle Tommy. Tommy was married to Rosie and they had two kids, Ginger and Andrew. To make this comprehensible, let me explain that Tommy and Rosie were very good friends of my parents, and I grew up with their kids, Ginger, who was one year younger than me, and Andrew who was three years younger. Being such close friends with my parents, Tommy and Rosie were referred to as Uncle Tommy and Rosie, not Aunt Rosie, just Rosie.

Uncle Tommy called me out of the blue. He had never called me personally. I answered the phone.

"Hello?"

"Hi there Jinni, how are you? It's Uncle Tommy," he said in a cheerful voice.

"What a surprise to hear from you. I am well; how are you and how is the family?" I asked.

"Oh, they are good, Jinni. But I am not calling to talk to you about the family. I was shopping you could help me out. I was wondering if you knew someone who could get me some pot.?" Uncle Tommy asked me as though I was just another one of his friends.

I believe my jaw fell to the ground, in shock.

"Well, um…….I am sure I could make a few calls and get some." I replied numbly.

"Ok, great Jinni! So, I hear you got your own place now. Where is it? I would like to come visit you in your new place and maybe by then you will have the pot for me." Uncle Tommy said.

My head was spinning; I could not comprehend this conversation.

"Ah…sure, Uncle Tommy it would be great to see you again."

As I was saying this, I was beyond numb.

"Give me a couple days. I am sure I can get some by the end of the week. So, let's just plan on Saturday afternoon. If anything changes, and I am not able to get some pot, I will let you know," I told him.

"Ok, great Jinni! Tell me your address and I will just plan on seeing you Saturday afternoon," Uncle Tommy said in closing.

I gave Uncle Tommy my address and we hung up. I had to sit down. I was shocked, as this conversation did not seem real. I then made a couple of calls to some not so frequent friends. I was able to find out who had some pot and set a day and time to pick some up.

The week flew by and Saturday arrived faster than I wanted it too. There was a knock at my front door as I was just cleaning up my apartment.

"Who is it?" I asked, already knowing.

"It's Uncle Tommy," I heard in reply. I opened the door and Uncle Tommy gave me a big hug. He had brown eyes and brown hair, was about five-five in height with an average build for a forty something year old. He had a very spunky personality, and always chewed gum.

"Hi there Jinni How have ya been? You're looking good!" he said with a twinkle in his eye.

I smiled and moved out of the doorway, as I said, "Thanks for visiting me in my new place. It's not big, but it's all right for now. And to answer your question, I am good Uncle Tommy. I had no problem getting you some pot." I was so nervous that my words just blended together.

"Oh, ok, great! How much was it?" He asked sounding pleased.

"Thirty-five dollars for a five ounce bag," I told him as I opened a kitchen cabinet where I had stored the bag of pot. I took out the bag of pot and placed it on the kitchen bar counter. He put his hand in his pocket and pulled out a lot of cash. He counted thirty-five dollars right in front of me placing it on the kitchen bar counter next to where the bag of pot lay as he helped himself onto one of the two bar stools I had set up at the kitchen counter. Uncle Tommy looked at me chuckling, with wild eyes and said, "So, how about it?" I froze in fear as I smiled nervously.

He put his hand in his pocket and pulled out a small packet of rolling papers. He took a paper out of the packet and put the packet back in his pocket. He opened the bag of pot and pinched a tablespoon's worth with his fingertips. He proceeded to roll a joint on my kitchen counter. I was standing there feeling as though I was in someone else's bad dream.

"Do you have a lighter Jinni?" he asked.

I stumble for my words, "Yes, um......I think I have one right here in the kitchen drawer." I remembered I had unpacked one and put it in the junk drawer. I opened the junk drawer, next to the refrigerator and grabbed the lighter and handed it to Uncle Tommy.

Uncle Tommy smiled and lit the joint. He took several hits off the joint and then offered me some. I felt paralyzed and in shock, but I played along with what was going on, and I took a few hits off the joint as well. I gave the joint back to Uncle Tommy as he was looking around the room.

"So, this is really a nice place you got here, Jinni." He got up from the stool and walked over to my futon where he sat down and made himself comfortable as he leaned back up against the wall.

"This is nice Jinni, why don't you come and sit with me? Let's watch some television together." I felt my stomach turn, and I felt like I wanted to throw up. I smiled and said with a lump in my throat, "Um...ok. Sure Uncle Tommy."

I turned the television on and sat on the edge of the futon. As Uncle Tommy sat back leaning against the wall, he looked at me and smiled. He leaned forward and pulled me back.

"Come sit closer Jinni," he said.

As he began to play with my hair he whispered, "You are so pretty." He proceeded to move his hands down to touch my breasts. I felt paralyzed; I was so very scared inside. I did not know what to do. I felt speechless and could not find the words to speak.

I finally mustered up the nerve to say, "Uncle Tommy, I don't think this is such a good idea." As if I had said nothing, he proceeded to grab my hands and placed them on his crotch. He unzipped his pants and grabbed my hands and used them to play with his penis. He leaned forward and began to kiss me.

"Take off your pants," he said.

"Um....I think I will keep them on," I said.

As he continued to hold my hands under his hands, making sure to stroke his penis, he said, "Suck my dick."

All I could think about was how to get out of there and how to make this stop. He moved his hands off mine, which were holding his penis and he put his hands on each side of my head and pulled my head down to suck on his penis.

When he was about to cum, I moved my face as I listened to him moan. When he was finished he asked to use the bathroom. I stood in my studio apartment, numb with fear, disgust and confusion. Uncle Tommy came out of the bathroom smiling.

"That was great Jinni I gotta go, but I will talk to you again real soon."

I smiled and walked him to the front door. I unlocked the door and watched him leave. I closed the door and locked it. I paced around my apartment for so long wondering what had just happened. I then sat on my futon and cried.

The relationship with Jeremy continued as usual. Jeremy on occasion, would visit my apartment and sometimes spend the night. Despite the fact that he was twenty three years old, he needed to get permission from his mother to sleep over at my place. As you can guess, he did not stay over very often. Bottom line, Jeremy was not nice to me nor was his family. Jeremy's mom was obsessive compulsive about keeping her house clean, and she treated her husband like her slave. She tried controlling anyone that came into her life. On several occasions, when visiting Jeremy's parent's house I would get to spend some time with his sister Claudine even though Jeremy's mother never left Claudine's side. I would secretly think, that despite Claudine's severe mental and physical handicap, she was the lucky one.

I had been in my apartment for about two months. My job was going well, and I had recently finished the six weeks of treatment at my gynecologist's office. I hadn't gotten my period in two months and just figured it was because of all the confusion and stress in my life. As time moved on, my landlord upstairs kept his distance and I had not heard from Uncle Tommy.

By the third month I had been in my apartment, I still hadn't gotten my period. I went to the store and bought a pregnancy test, brought it home, opened the box, and pulled out the instructions and the test stick. I reviewed the instructions then proceeded to pull down my pants and pee on the test stick just like the instructions had said to. I placed the stick next to the bathroom sink and went into the kitchen to get myself a snack.

I kept watching the time, as I had to wait fifteen minutes until the test was ready. I stayed away from the bathroom. I was scared to read it. Fifteen minutes went by too fast and I had to go back in the bathroom to check the results. I looked at the test stick and then I referred back to the instructions. According to the instructions, the test stick read positive.

I thought to myself, "No........this cannot be so."

I threw the test stick in the trash, left my house and went back to the store to purchase another pregnancy test. I came back home, ripped the pregnancy test kit open, walked straight into the bathroom, pulled my pants down and peed on the test stick again. I sat the test stick up on the kitchen sink again and went into the kitchen. Fifteen minutes later I went back into the bathroom. The results were positive.

I had not had a lot of sexual interactions with Jeremy. I was too disgusted with myself to want to be intimate with him. Besides, he was not nice and I just felt that I deserved to be treated poorly because I did not think much of myself. So I had to wonder whose baby I was pregnant with. Was it my upstairs landlord's STD baby?

Was it Uncle Tommy's, pot induced hand job baby?

Or was it my alcoholic, Doctor Jekyll-Mr. Hyde psycho boyfriend Jeremy's baby?

I made another appointment with my gynecologist, who confirmed that I was pregnant.

About this time, Jeremy began purchasing a lot of pot from his own sources. Jeremy had rolled a joint and lit it. As we sat on my futon in my apartment one day, I told him that I was pregnant. He smiled and said, "You are?" He proceeded to get up, face the wall and punch it. He turned to me and said in a mean tone of voice, "You are not keeping this baby. I am not ready to be a father, nor do I want to be one!" I began to cry; He opened the front door and slammed the door shut as he left.

Later, I called Jeremy to ask him if he was serious about what he said, but he would not answer the phone. Several days went by and I had not spoken to him. I thought, "Well, I am just going to keep this baby. It doesn't need to have a father. I can take care of it myself."

The next day Jeremy called me. He told me that I was <u>not</u> too keep the baby and the sooner I could make arrangements for an abortion, the better off our relationship would be. I felt powerless, as I called my gynecologist's office and spoke to the secretary. I told her that I was inquiring about pricing in regards to an abortion. I stumbled on my words and could not even say the word abortion without stuttering. I don't recall the exact price; however, I recall it was very expensive. I called Jeremy up later that day and told him the cost for an abortion. He told me that it was way too expensive and to look in the yellow pages for a facility that offered discounted abortions.

I did not say much to Jeremy other than, "Yeah…….thanks." I was numb and confused as I hung up the telephone. The next morning, I called in sick to work. I was nauseous, confused and could not focus on going into work that day. I needed to tell someone what I was dealing with and I thought I could muster up the courage to confide in my mom. It was early fall and I needed to drive to my mom's house.

My mom had bought me a used 1994 Toyota Corolla when I graduated high school.

Looking back, I recall when my Mom bought me that car. I recall coming home from school on a Thursday; I was in my senior year of high school. All my friends had cars and I didn't. I suppose I did not think I was worthy of getting a car considering it took three Driver's Ed tests before I passed and received my driver's license. I felt dumb and I had no confidence in myself.

I was so scared to take the Driver's Ed test because, technically, as the student, I would be 'judged' on how well I could drive. I had never done well with being 'judged'. Nevertheless, I knew I would eventually get a driver's license.

While in my room that day, I hadn't seen my cat, Cali, anywhere. I figured that she was probably just outside somewhere. My mom was home and I was in my room watching television.

Mom came to my room and stood in the door way. "I have been looking in the newspaper for a car for you, and I found one!" I smiled and asked,

"What kind is it Mom?"

"Oh......I cannot tell you that. It is a surprise!" she replied.

"Oh. Ok Mom." I replied curiously. Mom told me that after dinner we had to drive over to the car lot and sign the papers to purchase the car.

We had just finished eating dinner and gotten into my mom's car with me in the passenger seat and Mom driving, of course. The air felt cold and we were both quiet.

I turned to Mom and said, "I haven't seen Cali anywhere since I came home from school. I wonder where she is hiding."

My Mom, not being a fan of animals, looked at me and then back at the road.

"Well, Jinni, you know you don't take care of that cat. You don't clean the litter box.

She has been peeing constantly all over the rug in the office room. I had enough!

I took the cat to the vet she was sick and had the vet put her to sleep." She stated without feeling. Wow, I thought. Nothing like the feeling of being stabbed in the stomach.

Didn't my mom know how much I loved Cali? I didn't say a word. All I could think was that I really hated my Mom at that moment.

The sun was setting as we arrived at the car lot. It looked like a junk yard with stuff piled everywhere: cars, washer, dryers, toilets, tires, etc. The dealership 'office' was in a beat-up old RV trailer that sat in the middle of the lot. At this time in my life, I was out of touch with my feelings. However, I did not have a good feeling about this place.

We parked the car close to the RV trailer and Mom said,

"Ok, we are here. Let's go buy your car!" We got out of the car and walked over to the trailer. Mom opened the door of the trailer and called out,

"Hello?"

We heard a man say, in a smoker's voice, "Hi there, come on up."

My Mom walked up the three steps with me following close behind. The RV had this dark and dingy feeling about it and the smell of cigarette smoke was intense.

When we got to the top of the stairs, we both stood close to each other.

There was an extremely large white man about three hundred pounds, wearing a tank top, sitting at what appeared to be a kitchen table. He was drinking a Budweiser beer and had a lit cigarette sitting in an ash tray that was full of cigarette butts. He had a greasy face and his black greasy hair was slicked back on the sides of his head because the top of his head was bald. Beside him stood a thin man, wearing large rimmed, tinted glasses. He wore a diamond earring in his left ear. He had a full head of brown hair that was greased back, and he wore an oversized navy blue suit .

"Hi, I am Rosalyn, the lady that called you about the 1980 Cutlass Oldsmobile."

"Oh yes," the standing man commented.

"It's right back there," he said as he pointed eastward out the window.

My Mom and I peered out the window as she said,

"Well, its dusk out can we see the car outside?"

"Sure," the standing man said. The large man at the table said in a deep voice, "I've got the papers all ready to sign, when you get back." So, I followed Mom, who followed the man to the 1980, brown colored Oldsmobile.

As we stood at a distance, the man said, "See it's nice, isn't it? It has four doors, tinted windows, and it's in great shape. We are asking one thousand dollars for it."

My mom said, "Oh, I thought you were asking five hundred dollars."

"Well, considering we need to fine tune and make some minor repairs for you ladies, we are asking a thousand."

"Well, ok, but I only have five hundred dollars with me today," replied Mom.

"That's ok; you can give us the five hundred now, and pay for the other half when you come back to pick up the car."

"Well, that won't be for another week. I only have the five hundred until I get paid again next week," said Mom.

"Oh.......we'll be here then too," he said.

Something was really not right. This guy was very jittery. He really gave me a slimy feeling just by his body language and by the tone of his voice.

"Jinni do you want to walk over and see the car?" my Mom asked me.

"Oh....I um...can see it from here.....Yeah, it's nice," was all I could say because it was difficult to swallow. I smiled and glanced at my Mom, then at the man and then stared at the ground.

"Well, let's go back in the trailer and sign those papers!" he said.

We walked back in the trailer following each other in single file.

"Sit down," the very large man at the table said. I sat next to my mother as we sat across the small table from this large man.

"Ya got the money with ya?" he asked my mom looking at her like she was prime rib.

"Well, I have five hundred dollars with me," she said.

"Oh. Well, didn't Benny here tell you it's one thousand dollars? The newspaper made a mistake on the listing."

"Ah...yes, of course. I will have the rest of the money, one week from today for you."

The large man glanced over at the standing man named Benny. They stared at each other for a very long moment.

"Yeah, yeah, no problem lady, just sign here and give us the money."

"Well, what is it that I need to sign?" Mom asked.

"Oh, yeah, this is just some legality stuff we hand wrote up. You don't need to read it all.

Just sign it, give us the money and we will have your car waiting for you when you come back in a week.

"Oh, ok." My mom glanced over the hand-written document and signed. She opened up her purse and took five hundred dollars out of an envelope. She smiled as she handed the money over to the very large man.

"Here you go", my mom said. "My daughter and I will see you next week at the same time." She continued.

"Yeah, sure lady, see ya in a week." Benny said smugly.

We left and sat in silence most of the way home.

"So are you excited Jinni? It's a nice car you are getting." Mom said.

"Yup, it's a nice car," I said, in a flat tone of voice. Yet, I was thinking a million thoughts at the same time. I didn't like the car, I didn't like the sales people and the car lot gave me the creeps. I didn't know how to say all of this. I was afraid my mom would be angry with me if I told her how I really felt. I already knew that it didn't matter what I thought about anything. If Mom had an idea to do something or to buy something, not even the President could change her mind.

So, a week went by and Mom drove me down to the car lot. We drove to the address; however, nothing was there; only dirt on the ground and a vacant space.

"The car lot was here a week ago. I don't understand. Where is this place?" Mom fretted. I did not say a word. My stomach was in knots.

"Those thieves! They took my money! I am going to call the cops when I get home! Sorry, Jinni. I guess we are not getting you a car just yet." My mom said sounding frustrated.

I smiled and swallowed hard. I really don't know whatever happened after that, in regard to the car situation. All I can tell you is that the men took my mom's money and we never got the Oldsmobile.

About a month later, my mom told me she had found me another car. I recall going with my Mom on a Sunday to purchase this 1994 white Toyota Corolla. We drove up to a very nice home, rang the doorbell and out walked a very charming elderly man. He had very bright blue eyes; his hair was gray and parted to the side. He must have just returned from church as he was dressed in tan slacks and a very nice button down shirt.

"You must be here for the car," he said then looked at me and said,

"This must be for you. Ahhh, I remember when I got my first car. You're going to like this car. Come, let me show you."

Mom and I stood at the side of the drive way as he opened all the car doors and the hood and the trunk.

"I have been the original owner and I have taken care of this car.

There are only five thousand miles on it. You're sure, going to love this car," he said smiling at me.

My mom stood from afar. "How much?" she asked.

"Well, it says six hundred in the paper, but I will take five hundred for it," the elderly man said.

"Sold!" Mom said with a chuckle.

"Really?" I asked with a smile.

"Yep! Be safe and I will meet you at home." Mom pulled five hundred dollars out of her wallet and handed it to the man.

"Is there anything I need to sign?" she asked.

"Well, here is the title to the car. Just sign here that you are the new owners of the car," said the elderly man. Mom rummaged through her purse to find a pen. In the meantime, the elderly man looked at me and smiled as he handed over the keys to me.

I smiled back and said, "Thank you." I got in the car with a rush of feelings. I thanked my mom from the car. I started it up and drove away leaving Mom still in the driveway as she finished paying the elderly man. "See you at home Mom!" I said as I drove away with a huge smile on my face.

THE THREE OF LIFE
reminds me to think about;

1. **ATTITUDE** = Compliance is not self serving when you allow others to control your actions.
2. **LOVE** = Comes from honoring yourself first.
3. **HEALTHY RELATIONSHIPS** = Are not possible when your vision of reality is distorted.

You may believe that you are responsible for what you do, but not for what you think. The truth is that you are responsible for what you think, because it is only at this level that you can exercise choice. What you do comes from what you think.

-- A COURSE IN MIRACLES

Chapter Three

The Fender Bender

Now, that you know my car story we can get back to the original story.

It was a sunny day in August and I had been driving in bumper to bumper traffic when the car in front of me stopped short. I slammed on my brakes and hit the black Volvo in front of me.

A lady immediately got out of the car screaming,

"Are you crazy? I have kids and a baby in the car!!"

I stared at her and began sobbing.

I felt terrible that I hit the lady's car. I got out of my car to see the damage.

After she checked on her kids, she walked toward me and put her arm around me to console me. She looked at the back of her car where I had hit it and there was no apparent damage. My car on the other hand showed significant damage to the front lights. The owner of the Volvo said that she lived right around the corner and if I was ok to drive, that I should follow her to her house where her husband was home and could take a look at my car. As soon as I could gain my exposure and stop sobbing, I wiped off my wet face with my hands and got back in my car.

"When is this nightmare of a life going to end?" I asked myself allowed.

I followed the lady to her house. All I can remember is that her house was a colonial style home with very pretty green trimming on the outside. We both pulled into her drive way. I watched as she got the kids, an infant and a three-year old, out of the back seat of her car. She was carrying her baby to the front door as she turned toward my car and said, "Wait here." I got out and stood by the side of my car. Her husband came out to look at his wife's car then at mine. He smiled a warm smile and asked me if I was ok. I said I was. He took a closer look at my car and told me that I would need to take my car to me fixed. He suggested that we not call the insurance companies, and I nodded my head in agreement. I thanked him and got back in my car. He asked me if I was ok to drive, and I told him I wasn't going far and that I was ok.

I drove to my mother's house ten minutes away. I pulled into the circular driveway of the house which was a beautiful three-story colonial house with five bedrooms. My mom's car was not in the drive way. She did not use the two-car garage during the day, so I knew she was not home. I parked in front of the house and got out of my car. I unlocked the front door, and turned off the alarm in the entrance way. When you entered the house there was a bathroom to the immediate left and a closet to the immediate right. From there, the hallway went left and right.

To the right of the entrance sat the living room. It was a room that had an upright piano that sat to the left when you walked in the room. There were hard-wood floors and the walls were papered with the finest wall paper to match the antique furniture that filled the living room area. There was an antique, wood-trimmed, caramel colored couch that sat across from the piano. Behind the couch were curtains that covered a large elongated window. In between the couch and the piano was a fancy, marble antique coffee table top in a caramel color. The bottom of the coffee table was designed out of fancy antique wood. Sitting to the left and right of the coffee table were two antique chairs that matched the couch.

To the left of the entrance way, you had to walk past the basement door on your right before entering the kitchen. The kitchen was a very modern, large elongated room with an island in the center and a large bay window where the kitchen table was. To the left of the kitchen sat the family room/den. It was one step down from the kitchen. This room was cozy, with a brick fireplace, wood paneling on the walls, a hard-wood floor and a designer rug. It reminded me of a cozy room that you would see in a Colorado magazine.

To the right of the kitchen sat the dining room. It was filled with an antique wood dining set and breakfront which held Mom's delicate china.

The basement was what they called a half basement. It had a cement floor that my dad had painted corvette red and paneled wood walls. On one side, there was a closet that we used for a storage space. There was a laundry area and another door that led to the separate room my dad had made for a beauty salon for my mom to work in. The other side of the basement was an elongated room where we had family parties and where I would hang out with my friends or just hang out and listen to music.

I went up to my room that I grew up in and I just sat there on my bed, feeling numb, empty and without a thought. I sat there for a good half hour. Then my mom's house phone rang and I answered it.

"Hello?" I said.

"Hello? Jinni? What are you doing there?" It was Uncle Tommy.

"Um, I just passed by to visit my Mom."

"Oh, is your Mom home?" he asked.

"No," I said. "I have been here for a while and I don't know where she is."

"I am coming over," he said. And before I could say another word, he hung up.

Within twenty minutes the doorbell rang. I answered it already knowing it was him. I put on a smile and he greeted me with a big hug and tried to kiss me on the lips as I turned my face away.

"How ya doing Jinni? Any chance you gotta bag for me?"

"Um.....no Uncle Tommy. I, ah, didn't know I was going to see you today," I said.

"Ah that's ok. Do you know where your mother is?" he asked.

"No, she may be out shopping," I replied.

"Oh, well how about you show me your room?" He said.

"Ah......Uncle Tommy I don't think that is such a good idea. I mean, I don't know where my mother is and I don't know when she will be back." I stuttered my words.

"Oh, come on.......just show me your room," he said.

"Ah.....um......ok." I felt so unwilling and all I could think of was that I hoped my Mom would come home soon. We went up to my room and he pulled down his pants.

"Suck my dick like you did before," he ordered.

My stomach was in knots. My wrecked car sat in the circular drive way, my belly was full of a fetus and I just wanted my mom to come home.

Uncle Tommy placed his hands on his penis and stroked it. He then took his hands and placed them on either side of my head and forced my head down to his crotch.

"Suck on it like you did before," he said.

Numb and without feeling, I did as he told me to. When he was about to cum, I moved my face out of the way as he moaned and came all over himself. When he was finished he said, "Oh that was great! I need to go use the bathroom."

He walked downstairs to use the bathroom that was next to the front door.

In the meantime, I washed my hands and face in the upstairs bathroom and walked downstairs and into the kitchen.

When Uncle Tommy was finished in the bathroom, he called out for me, "Jinni?"

"I am in the kitchen," I said.

He walked into the kitchen and smiled and said, "So, you wanna do a blow?"

I looked at him strangely, not really sure what he meant.

"You know. Some blow………some white powder…………some cocaine."

I stared in disbelief. "I…..ah……No. I don't do that," I said. "Ah come on its fun!" Uncle Tommy said. He took a small bag of white powder out of his right pocket and poured it on the kitchen table as if I wasn't there. He then proceeded to make lines and snort the white powder cocaine.

"Ya wanna try some?" Uncle Tommy asked.

"Ah…no thank you. My mom should be home really soon." I said.

Uncle Tommy snorted the two lines of cocaine off the table. He stood up, wiped his nose with his left hand and then brushed the table off with his right hand.

"I will talk to you soon Jinni" he said as he gave me a wink of his eye and let himself out of the front door, closing it as he left.

I stood there for several long moments and stared at the closed front door. I felt numb and dead inside. I turned to go back into the kitchen where I had left my purse on the island countertop. I picked up my purse and without a thought, I left my mom's house.

She hadn't come home, while I was there. I didn't want to wait any longer and I just didn't have any strength or courage in me to tell her what I was going through. My mom was always so happy doing what she wanted to do, that anytime reality set in, it was time for her to go shopping, cook up an incredible recipe, or find something else to do rather than deal with reality. Besides, I figured she would probably completely deny hearing anything I would tell her. She didn't care anyway, I thought.

I set the house alarm and locked up. As I drove home to my apartment, tears streamed down my face. My reality was too much for me to even handle. As I was driving home, I passed a billboard that read "SAFE ABORTIONS" with a local number posted below it. I read the number and repeated it over and over again in my head until I stopped at a red light. I rummaged in my purse to find a pen and when I finally found one, I wrote the number on a rolled up gum wrapper that had been in my ashtray and stuffed it in my purse. I drove to my apartment and parked on the side drive way of the ranch style home. I sat in my car for a few moments, took a deep breath and got out of my car. I walked to the back of the house and downstairs to my apartment.

I unlocked the door, threw my purse on my futon, and glanced at the answering machine that was blinking on the kitchen counter. I pressed the playback button as I walked over to the kitchen cabinet to get a glass. When I opened the cabinet and grabbed the glass, I noticed there was black soot on the glass. I then lifted up a white dish that also had black soot on it. I looked down at the counter top and smeared my pointer finger across the counter top. My finger had black soot on it too. I said under my breath, "Gross! I suppose that's what happens when someone lives in a boiler room!"

The telephone messages were playing in the background. My mom called to see how I was doing and to tell me she was going to the flea market to go shopping. My dad had left a message telling me that if I didn't forget, I had a father and to call him some time.

My friend Nora had left a message about getting together to go to Friendly's for ice cream. That was it. No other messages. I picked up the phone as I thought about the messages. I could not think clearly. Having the phone in my hand and listening to the echoed dial tone, I reached for my purse. I dumped out its belongings onto my kitchen bar counter and rummaged through its contents until I found the gum wrapper with the phone number of the safe abortion clinic. I called the number and the message said that they were open from nine to four, Monday through Friday, and ten to two on Saturdays. And, if this was an emergency to dial 9-1-1. I looked at my alarm clock that sat on the basement/boiler room window sill and it read 5:20. I hung up the phone and just figured I would call them the tomorrow.

I intentionally collapsed back onto my futon. I laid there as I stared at the ceiling until it was dark. My mind was mixed with so many thoughts about my life, my relationships, my family, and my job. I got up and turned on the kitchen flood lights and then looked in the refrigerator for something to eat. I grabbed an apple, and shut the refrigerator door. I grabbed a knife from the utensil drawer, found the peanut butter in one of one of the cabinets and put it on the countertop. I opened another cabinet and grabbed a flat dish and placed it on the counter top next to the peanut butter. I turned on the kitchen faucet and rinsed the apple. Then I placed the still wet apple on the dish and sliced it. I threw the pits and the core of the apple into the trashcan that sat under the kitchen sink. I opened the utensil drawer again and grabbed a tablespoon, then pushed the drawer closed with the back of my hand. I opened the peanut butter jar, scooped out a table spoon of peanut butter and plopped it on the side of the dish that held the apple. I washed the knife and placed it in the drying tray. I fastened the lid on the peanut butter jar and placed it back in the cabinet. I tore off a paper towel from the paper towel roll, grabbed my dish and went back to sit on my futon.

I reached for the remote control that sat on top of the television. I turned on the TV and flipped through channels as I ate my apple, continuously dipping it in peanut butter. As I flipped through the channels, it was as if I wasn't even watching what was on the television. I thought to myself that I could not go to work the next day. I would have to call work and tell them that I was in a car accident and that I had to take my car to the mechanic. I thought about my pregnancy; I thought about what a loser my boyfriend was. Then my phone rang.

"Hello?" I said.

"Hi Jinni, what are you doing?" my mom's voice said.

"Oh, hi Mom. I, um...I'm just watching some television."

My mom chuckled as she asked, "So how was your day? What else did you do?"

"Mom," I was silent, trying to hold back my tears, "I was in a car accident today."

"Oh my goodness!!!! What happened to the car? Are you ok? Did anyone else get hurt? Did you get hurt? Why didn't you call me?" she asked all at once.

"Yes, I am ok, the car is banged up in the front some. I can't drive at night because the lights got smashed. I will have to take the car to a mechanic tomorrow.

"Oh. Okay. Jinni? Were you at the house today?" she asked.

"Ah...yeah. I was there. (I had to think up an excuse). I just wanted to see if you had any good leftovers in the refrigerator, but I didn't find any," I dumbly replied in an exhausted tone.

"Do you want me to go with you to the mechanics? Do you want me to follow you to the mechanic? Oh, what about your job? What mechanic are you going to anyway?" she asked all at once.

"Mom, I am really tired right now. I just want to get some sleep. I will call Jeremy in the morning and ask him who he uses. Thanks though. I will talk to you tomorrow Mom."

"Oh," my Mom said as I could feel the cold, tense air of rejection fill the room. "Well, I am here if you need me. Goodnight Jinni, Love you."

"Yeah......Goodnight Mom.............love you too." Those two words were so hard to say.

I hung up the phone and went into the kitchen where I threw away the paper towel and placed my dish in the sink. I went into the bathroom to take a shower. As I stood there in the midst of the shower, I closed my eyes and stood with my face in the water. After a few minutes I turned my back to the shower head. As the water sprayed on my back, I looked down at my stomach. I began to rub my stomach and cry. What a mess my life was in, was all I could think about. How could I bring this baby into this world, when my boyfriend was an alcoholic who had a Dr. Jekyll/Mr. Hyde personality? And besides, I was pretty sure the baby was not his, but my rapist landlord's. I turned the shower off, and dried myself off, and put on some comfortable pajamas. I walked over to my futon, turned off the lights, made myself very comfortable, snuggled in my blanket, left the television on low volume and went to sleep.

My alarm clock went off at five AM in the morning. I looked at the clock and knew I wasn't going into work that day. I had taken yesterday off work and had been in a car accident. Would they believe me when I called in to work today to take the day off again? I shut my eyes again and the snooze went off ten minutes later. I kept doing this until about seven thirty. I got up, showered, got myself ready, made some coffee and sat down at the kitchen bar counter to eat some cereal. I thought about all the things I had to do that day. For starters, I had to call Jeremy and ask him to refer me to a mechanic so I could get my car repaired. I also needed to call the safe abortion clinic number and schedule an appointment.

First I called work, I told them that I had been in a car accident and that I would not be back until Monday (considering it was a Friday). They did not seem very pleased with my calling in again. I felt so guilty calling in two days in a row, but what else was I supposed to do? I then called Jeremy at his work around 9:30.

"Hello…. 'Automotive Engine Repairs', can I help you?" said the male voice on the phone.

"Hi," I said with a smile. "Who is this?"

"This is Sal, can I help you?" said the male voice.

"Hi Sal, it's Jinni, Jeremy's girlfriend".

"Oh, yeah, hi Jinni. Hang on I will go get Jeremy for ya."

I said, "Thanks," as I heard the receiver being put down on a counter.

"Yeah, yello?" I heard Jeremy say.

"Hi Jeremy, it's Jinni." I said.

"Yeah, I know. What do you want?" he asked roughly. I felt like crying. I took a deep breath and reminded myself why I was calling him.

"I was in a car accident late yesterday afternoon and I was hoping since your dad works at a body shop, that maybe he could fix my car for me."

There was silence followed by a long pause.

"Do you know the number of your dad's repair shop?" I continued.

"Ah yeah, let me go get the number, hang on." Jeremy said roughly as I heard the phone drop down on the counter. In a few moments he came back and said,

"The number is 212-788-9297 but don't expect to get your car fixed for free. You will have to pay my dad."

"Oh, ok." I said. He hung up the phone as I was about to say thanks, so I hung up the phone on my end and sat on the bar stool just staring at the wall thinking. Why didn't he ask me if I was ok or ask if I had gotten hurt in the car accident? Why didn't he ask me about the baby? I swallowed hard. I grabbed the piece of paper on the bar kitchen counter that had the phone number of the safe abortion clinic. I picked up the telephone and dialed the number.

"Hello?" shouted a scratchy monotone female voice.

"Hello," I said trembling under my breath.

"I was wondering where you are located," I continued.

"We are located on the north side of Learner Avenue, diagonally across from the 7-11 store," the scratchy monotone voice said.

"Oh. Ok. I know where that is. I........um............" stuttered feeling terrified, "I need to make an appointment," I said unwillingly.

"How pregnant are you?" asked the monotone female voice.

"I, um....um....just one and a half months, I think," I said feeling like a child myself.

"Well, if you are going to have an abortion, now is a good time because we cannot do abortions if you are three or more months pregnant."

"Oh,".........I said, feeling so very scared and not wanting to go through having an abortion. "Um............let me think about this some more and call you back," I said in hesitancy." Click went the other line as I sat in my kitchen with the telephone receiver still up against my ear listening to the echoing of the dial tone.

Well, I don't want to have an abortion anyway, I thought to myself. I don't need Jeremy to have this baby! I continued to repeat this in my mind knowing very well that I was terrified.

I called the phone number that Jeremy gave me for his dad's car repair shop.

"Hello..........'Chevy Auto body,' can I help you?" spoke a male voice.

"Hi, can I please talk to Mr. Moreau?"

"Sure hold on", said the male voice.

"Hello? Who is this?" I recognized Mr. Moreau's voice because he had a very thick French accent. I immediately got choked up and couldn't find my words as I wanted to cry. Mr. Moreau, unlike his slave driving wife, was a very kind, hardworking man. I felt bad for him, to be married to such a monster.

"Hi," I said holding back tears. "Um.........this is Jinni, Jeremy's girlfriend. I was in a car accident yesterday and I was hoping you could take a look at my car and fix it at your shop." I trembled with fear that he might say no.

"Well, I don't know. If you can still drive it, I can maybe take a look at it here at the shop." He said in hesitation.

"Sure, Mr. Moreau, thank you. Just tell me the address of the shop and I can bring it by tomorrow. You are open on Saturdays aren't you?" I said.

"I will tell Jeremy to drive you here tomorrow," he said. My stomach was in knots. I did not want to have to depend on Jeremy because his personality scared me so.

"Ok, thank you Mr. Moreau," I said and hung up. I immediately called Jeremy at work again. He answered the phone.

"Hi Jeremy, it's Jinni again."

"You know I am at work. You can't keep calling me here while I am working," he said in an annoyed tone.

"Sorry. I, um....just wanted to let you know that I spoke to your dad and he wants you to take me and my car to his shop tomorrow," I said this with feeling fear and expecting rejection.

"Damn it! He knows I work on Saturdays! Yeah, I guess I will talk to my boss about working half a day tomorrow," Jeremy said still annoyed.

"Thanks," I said.

"Yeah, ok. I will call you after work," Jeremy said as he quickly hung up the telephone.

Jeremy called me after work and told me to drive over to his parents so we could go hang out at the local pub place. I told him that I could not drive my car at night because the lights had been smashed. So he told me to come over to his parents while it was still light out and I could just sleep on the couch in the basement. I was so sick of going to this pub. It was boring and I did not like to drink, nor did I like the person Jeremy became when he drank. I especially hated going over to his parent's house. When he asked me this, my stomach immediately knotted up like tangled yarn. Without a will or, a voice of my own, I said ok. I hung up the phone, grabbed a few toiletries, pajamas, and clothes for tomorrow. I locked up my apartment and got in my car and drove over to Jeremy's parent's house. I already hated being there. We had dinner with his parents and his mother told us that we were not allowed to go out. So the entire family watched a movie in the downstairs living room. When the movie was over, Jeremy's mother kept mumbling under her breath, "She better not make a mess of my bathroom. She better clean up after herself. Why is she staying here? Her and that stupid car!"

"I will open up the sofa bed for you," she said with an annoyed undertone.

"Oh Ok. Thank you," I said not sure why all of a sudden she was being nice.

She opened up the sofa bed and put clean sheets on it. Then she said,

"Everybody is going to sleep now. If you have to use the bathroom, use it now because it makes a loud noise and we don't want to be awakened from it in the middle of the night."

"Yes, of course," I said with a grimace on my face. I walked upstairs and used the bathroom, making sure I hadn't moved anything out of place. I went back downstairs to sleep on the sofa bed. I tossed and turned all night; feeling so very unwelcome there.

The next morning, I got up early as I heard Mr. Moreau getting ready for work, not to mention the fact that Mrs. Moreau screamed down to me,

"Jinni get up! It's the morning time and you need to leave soon."

I got up instantly. I immediately cleaned up the sofa area, making the sofa bed as neat as it could be and folding it back to its original sofa position. I looked around hoping I did not shed any of my hair on the couch or on the rug. I shook my head as I did this, and mumbled under my breath, "I can't believe I am doing this; this is insane. I am terrified of this woman."

I went upstairs and Mrs. Moreau made everyone French toast. I suppose it was a good breakfast meal, although I felt like I was swallowing cement with each bite. When breakfast was over, Jeremy drove me in my car as we followed his dad to his work.

THE THREE OF LIFE
reminds me to think about;

1. **ATTITUDE** = During times of darkness, it's important to stay strong and believe that there still exists a small flame of light.

2. **LOVE** = We are each very special and created in Gods image with Love.. The trials we go through are not always understood. With faith there is always love that helps us to continue to walk forward knowing that there is a light ahead that burns bright.

3. **HEALTHY RELATIONSHIPS** = The healthiest of relationships begins with ourselves. However, when this relationship seems to be the most difficult, so is all the other relationships in our life. If the people we attract are reflections of ourselves—Yet, we find that we don't like whom we've attracted, then it is time to stop where we are at and take a significant look within and re-evaluate our perception of reality and our thoughts.

"The trouble with using experience as a guide is that the final exam often comes first and then the lesson."

~ANONYMOUS

Chapter Four

A Numb Existence

At Mr. Moreau's auto body shop, the mechanics there were evaluating my car. They told me the repairs would cost about six hundred dollars. I had no choice but to have my car fixed and pay for it. The bigger problem was that I would not be able to pay my next month's rent. That evening when I was home in my apartment, I called my friend Nora and told her what happened to my car. I told her that I would need to move back home with my mom because I was unable to pay the next month's rent. I told her I hoped that my landlord would understand.

Nora always looked at situations in a diplomatic way. She commented, "Well, if your landlord gives you a hard time, just tell him you will call the police on him because it is against the law to have someone live in the boiler room. There are health hazards to this and he will be arrested!" She had me convinced.

My goodness I thought, if she only knew my entire story and what I was going through. I wondered if she would still be my friend. After I hung up with Nora, I called Reed, my landlord.

"Hi Reed, this is um, Jinni, your tenant downstairs."

His tone of voice was very cold and unfriendly, "Hi." I continued to speak in a humble tone of voice. "Reed, um....I was in a car accident," I said expecting some empathy. He was silent, so I continued to speak after a long pause.

"I paid you first and last month's security deposit. I had to pay to have my car fixed, so please use the last month's rent that I gave you to pay this next month, and I will be moving out by the end of the month."

He then, responded frantically, "You can't do that! You have to pay the rent!"

"Um....I did," I responded, trying to stay calm.

"This is unacceptable, you have to pay the rent or I am going to contact a lawyer friend of mine!" he threatened me.

My blood began to boil, as I trembled in fear. "Good," I said.

"Good," I continued after a brief hesitation; "Call your lawyer friend. Call the police even.

The fact that you are renting out your boiler room is against the law. It's a health hazard."

I kept hearing Nora's words repeat in my head as he hung up the telephone first.

Early October was my nineteenth birthday. This year was unlike most because it seemed to be such a blur. Jeremy had taken me out to dinner for my birthday and another night; my dad took me out to dinner. Yet another night, my mom took me out for dinner in honor of my birthday. So it was like having three birthdays in one. Still no one knew about my pregnancy, my dealings with my landlord, my past health issues, or the infrequent visits from Uncle Tommy. At nineteen years of age, all I could think of was; "Why me?" My life seemed to be such a secret mess. I wondered how to erase my life and start over.

About mid-October, I tried to talk with Jeremy about keeping the baby. I recall having this discussion while he was driving us back to my apartment. He was yelling and spitting as he told me that there was no way that he would let me keep this baby. He specifically told me that he was not ready to have kids, nor did he want any children to begin with. I cried and would often speak to my baby in my mind. Assuming the baby could be a boy, I called him Anthony. All I could do was constantly apologize to baby Anthony, as I felt such shame, blame, guilt and uncertainty. Jeremy told me that if I did not call and schedule the abortion, that he would call and schedule it for me. As usual, I gave in to him and I called when we got back to my apartment. Jeremy stood there in my apartment watching me call and schedule the appointment. The earliest I could make it for was the first week in November and I knew by then I would definitely be almost three months pregnant.

At the end of October, my mom helped me move back into her house that was being foreclosed on. I had nowhere else to go although I could have moved in with my dad.

Then my mom would have been alone. I felt torn; nevertheless, I moved back in with my mom. Looking back during this time in my life, I really hated my mother and the way she lived her life as a single mom. She acted like she was eighteen again, and I couldn't stand it. On the other hand, my Dad whom I saw infrequently was someone I confided in more than anyone else at times. Although every now and again, I felt he betrayed my trust when his tone of voice would change from that of a friend to that of a disciplinarian.

The day had come for me to get the abortion. I had made the appointment for a Saturday morning. I remember Jeremy picked me up early that morning. As we drove to the clinic, I repeated over and over again in my head,

"I do not want to do this; I do not want to have an abortion. I do not want to do this; I do not want this abortion. I want to keep my baby Anthony, but I don't know how to. Will he ever forgive me for not standing up for myself and for him? I do not want to do this."

As we drove to this place, there were people marching and holding picket signs that said, "Stop Abortion!" I began to cry.

Jeremy noticed and snapped at me. "You just stop that! You are going through with this!"

We parked on the side of the brick building. We had to walk around to the back of the building and walk down the stairs to what seemed like a white cellar door. We opened it and walked into a small white, square room with six chairs. There were several girls already waiting there. There was an office window and a door next to it. I unwillingly walked up to the office window as Jeremy stood there.

"Hi....I......um......am here for an abortion." I said.

"Hi. What's your name?" said the pale blonde haired girl behind the window.

"Jinni," I stuttered and spoke under my breath.

"Jinni Montgomery," I said.

"Ok, yes, just have a seat and I will call you back after these girls have gone first."

She said this as if we each had a number. Jeremy looked at me and said,

"It will be ok but I am leaving. When should I come back for you? Ask them how long it's going to take."

I felt like I wanted to throw up. I turned away from him and walked back to the lady behind the office window and asked her how long I would be there.

"Well, there are five girls ahead of you, so maybe about three hours. Once we get you in the room, it will be quick though. But you have to pay me first."

Jeremy heard her and he gave me a grimace and asked coldly,

"How much is this?"

"Two hundred dollars," I said in unison with the girls behind the office window.

"Oh.........well, I will have to write you a check" he said like it was just another bill to pay.

"Ah, we take cash only," the girl said smartly.

"Ok, I have to go to the bank and get the money. I'll be back." With that he left the room.

I sat in one of the sturdy, yet uncomfortable chairs in the room with these girls. I looked at each one of them. Three of the girls were white and the other two were African American. They each looked like everyday girls like me. But there was this one girl who sat to the left of me. She had long brown straggly hair and wore blue short shorts and a white button down shirt that had a rugged look to it. It wasn't what she wore that made me wonder about her, it was the expression on her face that held my curiosity. She wore makeup to brighten her very pale yet pretty face; yet, in her eyes I saw so much pain and sadness. I wondered what her story was. Then again, we were both sitting in the same room for the same reason. I sat there for three and a half hours. Jeremy came back finally with the money and paid the girl. He told me he would be back in another hour or so to check to see if the abortion was finished. Shortly after Jeremy left, the girl from behind the office window opened the door.

"Jinni Montgomery? You're next" she said.

Those words sounded very thick as they echoed in my head. She took me to the patient room which was a very small walk-in closet like white room. There was a white sheet over what may have been a cot with stirrups attached to it. Diagonally across was a table with instruments to be used by the doctor whom I still had not met. The girl told me to get undressed and lay down on the table because the doctor would be in shortly. She shut the door as she left, and I undressed, crying and mumbling, over and over again. "I do not want to do this,".

I laid down as tears streamed down the sides of my face into my hair. Then the door opened.

As the door creaked opened, I gasped for air as a very large man with a Hawaiian a complexion, wearing a white coat entered. I guessed him to be at least three hundred pounds standing at a height of six feet. I was even more terrified and I just wanted to get up and run. Yet before I knew it, this large man placed a mask on my face. When I awoke, he was out of the room and my legs had been covered by a white sheet. I sat up and looked around. Over to my right, there was a metal table standing in front of the bed I lay on. I almost passed out as I gasped for breath staring at several doctors' tools that still had blood on them. It felt like such a nightmare. I had wondered what happened and if I could leave. I got up and dressed myself. My stomach felt raw inside. I walked out of the room slowly. There was no one in the waiting room, and no one in the office area. There was a very eerie feeling I felt as I left the office, walking up the stairs into the sunlight.

Jeremy had been sitting there in his truck. I walked over to the passenger side, opened the door and climbed in the truck.

"Hey, how's it going? Are ya hungry? Want to get something to eat?" he asked as if it were just another day.

I could barely speak. I felt so dead inside.

"Just take me home," I mumbled under my breath.

We drove in silence on the way home. When we got to my mom's house, I got out of the truck without saying a word. I closed the truck door and just walked toward the front door without saying anything to Jeremy. He said nothing in return. As I unlocked the front door, I heard the truck rumble away.

My mom was busy working in the basement. I did not even say hello. I went up to my room and put on my pajamas and went to bed. I got up late in the evening and made myself some Ramen noodles I had found in the kitchen pantry. My mom was in the kitchen, and she had asked me what was wrong. I told her I wasn't feeling well and that I must have picked up a stomach bug or something. I told her that I just wanted to sleep it off. Little did she know what I was going through.

My stomach really hurt, and I figured it was just from the abortion. After eating I went back to sleep and did not awaken until the morning. When I got out of bed, my stomach was cramping terribly. I did not know what to do or whom to call. Jeremy did not care about me, and I had not told anyone else. My mother and I were not seeing, eye to eye on most things at this time in our lives, so it was better to just keep my distance from her. Yet, I really needed someone's help. I thought about contacting you, Ms. Lisa. But it had been so long since we spoke that I kind of thought, you would not remember me anymore. So, I called my dad.

"Hello. Martin Montgomery here," Dad answered.

"Hi Dad, it's me, Jinni," I said with as much strength as I had left.

"What's wrong? What's the matter!? I can hear it in your voice. What's the matter?" he nervously responded.

"Can I come over?" I asked in desperation.

"Sure," he said without a pause. "But what's the matter Jinni?" he continued to question.

"I um..........my stomach kind of hurts," I said, trying not to tell him my story on the telephone.

"Well, I am here for you, come on over." He responded concerned.

I grabbed my purse. I felt so sick that I keeled over with stomach cramps. I left the house without even saying goodbye to Mom. I got in my car and drove to my dad's house, which was about fifteen minutes away. I pulled in the driveway, parked my car and walked up to the front door where I rang the doorbell. Dad opened the door with a quizzical expression on his face.

"Come on in, what's the matter? You look terrible." He said with fear in his eyes.

My dad's house was nice. Upon entering, there was the living room off to the right and as you continued to walk forward there was a very large kitchen. The entire home had a southwestern accent style too it. To the right of the kitchen, there was a step down into the den/television room area. I walked over and sat on the couch. I grabbed the blanket on the couch and laid back, covering myself. When the doorbell had rung, dad's girlfriend Myrna (at the time), came in and sat down as Dad stood in front of the couch asking me what was wrong.

"I am afraid to tell you," I said to my dad.

"You can tell me anything, I have told you that before," he said reminding me. I paused and the silence in the room scared me. I took a deep breath and said, "I, um, was pregnant. I had an abortion yesterday at this basement-like clinic. My stomach really hurts today."

My Dad did not scold me as I thought he might. Instead, he asked where this clinic was and how I heard about it. I did not say much other than to mention the billboard sign.

He was quiet for a moment; a very long moment.

"Come on, get up and get in the car. I am taking you to the hospital."

His girlfriend looked at him and said, "Do you think they used dirty surgical tools?"

Dad responded without looking her way, "I wouldn't be surprised."

I got up and followed my dad and Myrna and got into the car. They drove me to the emergency room at the local hospital. I don't remember much other than telling my mom and friends who visited me over the next five days that I had a stomach virus. The truth of the matter was that I had a terrible infection in my uterus. Doctors at this hospital, believed just as my dad, that this back door clinic did not use sanitary tools and procedures. It appeared they seemed to be using the same utensil/tools for each girl, one after the other, who came in for an abortion. Doctors had me hooked up to an IV which was a mixture of all the strongest antibiotics they had.

I had called work from the hospital to tell them I wasn't well. I told them that I was in the hospital and that I would call them and let them know when I would be back to work again. After a week in the hospital, my stomach felt better. Yet, my mind felt screwed up. I felt terrible for aborting this baby. My so called boyfriend rarely called or visited me. Yet, I needed to be close to someone and feel loved. I called Jeremy and told him that I really needed to be held. When he came to visit me when I was back at my mother's house, he held me, but it was such a cold feeling. As his hug felt cold and unloving, as if he was doing me a favor.

The following week, I went back to work. After a few days of working there, I questioned my integrity. "What was I doing there?" I asked myself. "Why was I there?" I did not want to be there anymore. Not thinking clearly, and constantly blaming myself for having an abortion, I kept thinking of myself as disgusting. I kept going over in my mind that my rapist landlord with the STD's was the father. I sometimes thought about how Uncle Tommy would call me from time to time asking me to get him some pot. I just could not keep my head on straight and control the repetitive static thinking. I told my boss I was quitting. I believe they were as shocked as I was, yet I could not think clearly or grasp the concept of my reality.

I was home at my mom's house one evening when she received a distressing call. I could tell in her tone of voice.

"Oh, a huh.....a huh...oh, I am so sorry, is there anything I can do? Anything you need?

Ok. When and where is the funeral? Ok, I know where that is. Ok.......see you there." When Mom got off the telephone I could tell she was crying.

"Uncle Tommy's sister-in-law, Jackie, passed away from the cancer." She blurted out.

"Oh, I am so sorry, Mom. I really liked her." I sympathized.

"The funeral is tomorrow night. You will need to go. It's the right thing to do," she stated.

"Ah.....sure Mom, yeah, ok," I replied as my stomach turned and my throat felt choked up. I knew I would see Uncle Tommy there.

The next evening I drove with my mother to the funeral home to pay my respects. There were a lot of people there. It was a lovely service inside a chapel room where the closed casket sat in the front of the room. Sitting next to it was a very large picture of Jackie. I recall many of Jackie's relatives got up to speak. It was very touching. When the service was over, I remember giving my condolences to many of these people unrelated to me with whom I grew up with.

I walked out of the chapel room into the lobby area of the funeral home. As I was walking down the corridor, Uncle Tommy was approaching me followed by Uncle Frank.

Uncle Tommy smiled at me and winked. "Hey there," he said. He turned to Uncle Frank and said in a sinister tone, "She is my favorite one of them all." I wanted to run, I wanted to scream, I wanted to throw up. I could not understand any of this. Uncle Tommy's sweet sister-in-law, Jackie had just died and he was bragging to Uncle Frank about me being his 'favorite.' Of course all I could think of was that he meant I was his favorite slut.

Looking back now, I realize what a victim I was. I was nineteen, one year older than, Uncle Tommy's daughter. How disgusting was that? I always liked his wife, but she had no idea what her husband, her 'Tommy', was up to behind her back. My goodness if she only knew!

THE THREE OF LIFE
reminds me to think about;

1. **ATTITUDE** = When we loose our ground and have no self control, life becomes a struggle and nothing makes sense.
2. **LOVE** = Loving ourselves first becomes the hardest thing to do.
3. **HEALTHY RELATIONSHIPS** = Even when we feel alone at our darkest times, there is always someone to turn too for support.

"Beware the flatterer; He feeds you with an empty spoon."
~ COSINO DE GREGRIO

"When I looked in the mirror, my reflection told me that I am a kind and trusting soul. Yet, I am the most gullible human being I know."
~ LISA EVA GOLD

Chapter Five

A light is smothered by the Comfort of Darkness

One afternoon, I was out shopping at the grocery store. I was standing in line to check out, when I noticed that standing behind me was a good looking, kind-faced, guy about my age. He was probably about 5'6" in height, had brown eyes and, wore brown hair that was styled like Eric Estrada wore in the television show, "Chips." We started chatting, as we stood waiting in this long check-out line. We clicked right away; our conversation was just easy going and comfortable. He asked for my phone number and even though I knew I had a boyfriend, I gave him my number. I did feel terribly guilty however. He checked out after I did, yet the time that we shared chatting in line felt like eternity, although in reality it was only a few minutes.

That night at home the phone rang. My mother had answered the kitchen phone while I had been up in my room painting my toe nails. As I contemplated my life and how miserably stuck I truly felt, my mom called up to me from downstairs, "Jinni! The phone is for you." I picked up the telephone in my room and I could hear my mom hang up her line.

"Hello?" I said.

"Hi Jinni," the friendly male voice said.

"It's Andy, the check-out line guy you met today."

Suddenly, my energy shifted and I lit up like a Christmas tree. "Hi Andy," I said feeling refreshed. "How are you doing? Get everything you needed at Pathmark?" I asked.

The conversation went in every direction conversations go when two people are very interested in each other. We could have talked all night; however, after three hours, I told him that my mom wanted me off the phone. I also knew very well that I had better get off the telephone because if Jeremy was trying to call me, I needed to be available.

However, at the conclusion of our conversation, Andy asked me to go out with him the next night. I was so nervous and I knew that Jeremy would literally kill me if he knew I was even talking to another guy. But despite my horrid reality I could not say no to Andy.

He was so very sincere and considerate; I did not know how to say no.

On the night that we were scheduled to go out, I lied to Jeremy and told him that my mom needed some help packing. Her house was in foreclosure and she had to make plans to move. I figured it was the perfect white lie. He believed me, yet I felt horrible about lying.

I was downstairs in my mother's hair salon fixing my hair when I heard the rumbling of a motorcycle outside. The doorbell rang and I turned the light off in the hair salon and ran upstairs, switching the basements lights off as well. As I walked to the door, I felt very nervous. All I could think about was the dread that I felt about lying to Jeremy. If he only knew that I was going out on a date with another guy, I feared even imagining what he would do to me.

I opened the front door with a smile on my face to hide my internal turmoil. To my surprise Andy stood there with a dozen red roses. I wanted to cry. I couldn't remember the last time anyone had bought me flowers.

"Hi, wow! Thank you so much!" I said as he handed the roses to me with a big smile on his face. He paused and looked at me sincerely and said, "You look beautiful." His words came right from the heart and I could have just cried my eyes out right then and there. Yet, I clenched my jaw and gritted my teeth.

"Come on in," I said.

We walked into the kitchen where I put the roses in a vase and arranged them. Andy just stood there and watched with a smile on his face.

"I am glad you like the roses. They are beautiful like you. What would you like to do this evening? Have you eaten dinner?" His words were genuine.

I was trembling inside wondering what Jeremy would think. Oh, how I feared him. And standing in front of me was this very sincere guy.

"I.......ah.........don't know. I haven't really eaten but I am not that hungry," I stuttered.

"Well, let's go for a ride on my bike and then maybe you'll be hungry. I know a great little pizza joint," he said.

I smiled. "Ok. That sounds good to me."

We left my mom's house; I locked the door as I turned to admire his Harley Davidson motorcycle. "Have you ever ridden before?" he asked.

"Well, I rode on my cousin's scooter as a kid, does that count?" I replied with a chuckle.

He did not answer but just smiled.

"Well, a motorcycle is a bit bigger than a scooter. Let me show you the bike and then you can get on and feel safe riding as you sit behind me. Ok, for starters, this is where the chrome pipes are. They get extremely hot and if you are not careful you will burn your leg. I learned that after having burnt my own leg. So, be careful. Now, I am going to sit in the front and you just sit behind me and hold on tight. Here is a helmet to wear; it will keep the wind out of your eyes."

He explained all this in an even toned, caring voice which was something I really was not used to. I really did not know how to react.

I stood there and smiled as he showed me his bike and handed me the black helmet.

We each put on our helmets and fastened the straps. He got on the bike and started it up. I could hear his muffled voice through our helmets,

"Careful getting on, and hold on tight!"

I got on the bike and put my arms around his waist. I felt terribly guilty, as though I was committing a crime. It had to be around four in the afternoon when he came to pick me up. We drove on his bike for about a half an hour, and all I could think about was what would happen if Jeremy passed us on the road. Would he recognize me? I wondered if anyone Jeremy knew was driving by and if they would be able to tell that it was me. Would they tell Jeremy that they saw me with another guy? My stomach quivered and my mind raced through these repetitive fearful thoughts which kept me from enjoying the moments that I was truly living.

We pulled into this little shack called 'The Pizza Joint'. He turned off the bike, put down the kick stands with the heel of his right foot, and got off the bike first. He took his helmet off and reminded me again about the chrome pipes being too hot, especially after riding. I got off the bike and took my helmet off also.

We left the helmets on the seat of the bike and went inside. We walked into what looked like a log cabin on the inside. There were about eight square tables with those red and white checkered table clothes on them scattered around the room. To the immediate left of the entrance, was a wood bar that sat in front of the kitchen window. I did not see the kitchen, but I imagined that the kitchen had to be the size of a walk-in closet.

I followed Andy as he walked in like he owned the place. We were greeted by a voice from the left that said in a friendly voice, "Hi Andy."

Andy responded, "Hey Mike, how are you doing today?"

We sat down across from each other at one of the square tables. There was only one other couple sitting far in the back of this small pizza joint.

"Are you hungry now?" Andy asked me with a smile.

"Sure," I replied with a smile.

"What is your favorite Italian food to order?" Andy asked.

"Ah…pizza," I smiled in response.

"Sounds good to me," he said with a smile.

"Sit right here and I will go order for us".

I was amazed at how nice this guy was to me. I smiled as I watched Andy as he went to the bar to order two slices of pizza; however, I still felt guilty.

When Andy came back he said, "Is cheese pizza ok? I did not even ask you if you wanted anything on your pizza."

I smiled, "Yes, cheese pizza is perfect."

I sat there with turmoil, guilt, and shame all churning at the same time within. Who was I to deserve such kindness? I couldn't remember the last time that someone was truly interested in what I did or didn't like. I felt so ugly and dirty on the inside. Why couldn't my life be different? Why couldn't I just have a simple life with a kind boyfriend like this?

I pondered these questions.

"Have you ever been here?" I am so glad you are here with me.

"I come here from time to time. The pizza is great here and my cousin Mike runs this pizza joint. He's not always here though," Andy said looking at me intently.

"Um..........no, I have never been here. I love pizza, so I am looking forward to eating good tasting pizza." I said with a smile to hide my churning interior.

Andy sat there and smiled as he looked at me with admiration.

"This is fun. Hey, let me go and check to see if our pizza is ready." Andy got up and as I watched him walk over to the bar counter to pay for the pizzas, he turned his head in my direction and asked, "What would you like to drink?"

"Coke," I responded. Andy paid Mike at the register that sat in the corner up against the entrance wall of the bar counter.

Andy came back with a green tray in his hands. There were two slices of cheese pizza on white picnic paper plates and the drinks were in the tall oversized red plastic cups.

"Well, here we are," Andy said as he handed me over my drink and then my pizza."

He removed his plate and drink and sat it on the table and placed the tray on the table beside us.

"Can I get you anything else? Some cheese or hot pepper?" he asked.

"This looks and smells really good. I might like some grated cheese," I responded.

Andy got up again and grabbed the tall cheese shaker from off the bar counter and placed it in front of me. He sat down and as I put some cheese on my already cheese pizza he took the first bite of his slice of pizza.

"Mmmmm.....this is good stuff!"

I smiled as I shook my head in agreement. I put the cheese shaker down and took a bite of my slice of pizza.

We talked about different things, like what we do for work and what we aspired to be and about our families. Andy told me he was in the Army and that it was good to be home with his family. We talked for at least two hours before we got up and left. Before we left, he looked at me with such sincerity and told me how good it was to have met me. I felt like I was a million miles away from deserving his respect and appreciation. I did not know how to respond.

It had to have been close to seven in the evening as he was driving me back home on his bike. I felt safe until he pulled into the parking lot of the park down the street from where I lived.

He got off the bike and took his helmet off. He smiled and said,

"The weather is so great out and I don't want our time to end. I thought we could just sit here in the park and talk for a while longer before I take you home," he said sincerely.

I felt so very nervous, yet I had begun to feel safe and I did not know what to expect from this point on. I took off my helmet while still sitting on the bike, and as I got off the bike, I leaned nervously to my right and burnt my inner right ankle on the heated chrome pipe.

I let out a small yelp, but held back from making it a big deal. Andy turned to look at me and could tell that I burnt my leg.

"Oh, my goodness, are you ok? See I told ya that those pipes are hot. Well, I thought we could just sit on the benches over there and talk, but it's probably a better idea to get you home and get some ice on that burn," he said endearingly.

Andy put on the helmet he had been holding and got back on the bike and started it up.

"Ready?" I heard him shout through the helmet.

"Ready!" I shouted back.

He pulled into my drive way and parked. We both got off the bike and removed our helmets.

"Well, it has been a really nice first date, minus the burn on your leg. You should probably get inside and put some ice on that. As much as I don't want to leave you, I should go for now. But I can't wait to see you and spend time with you again."

He smiled, and kissed me on the cheek. I did not know how to respond to such respect. He fastened the helmet I had used to the back of the bike. He put his helmet on, got on his bike and left. I stood there in awe of such respect and kindness, as I watched him drive off.

Back to my nightmare life, was what went through my mind. The front door was unlocked, and I found my mother cooking in the kitchen.

"Hey Mom," I said blankly.

"Hi Jinni, How did it go?" She asked curiously.

"Um, it was nice. He is very nice."

"How do you know of him again?" she asked.

I mumbled, "Never mind Mom, I have a boyfriend already. I feel like I just cheated on Jeremy by going out with this guy Andy," I expressed with guilt.

"Well, you are not married. And by the way, Jeremy called for you," she replied firmly.

"No, I am not married yet—Jeremy called?" I repeated in a panic. "Where did you tell him I was?" I continued to panic.

"I didn't talk to him; he left a message on the answering machine," she replied as she was busy mixing together some ingredients for big party she was throwing.

My mind went into panic mode as I walked straight to the freezer to take out some ice that I wrapped up in a paper towel. I said nothing else to my mom, grabbed the cordless phone from off the counter and detoured out of the kitchen up to my bedroom. I flopped myself down on my bed and put my right leg up on the bed and placed the ice on my inner right ankle.

I sat there scared to call Jeremy. I asked myself what I was going to tell him. I couldn't tell him where I was. What about my leg? When I see him again, it will be so obvious that I burnt my leg. I was a bundle of nerves. I dialed the phone and he answered.

"Hi Jeremy, how are you?" I asked sweetly.

"Where have you been?" he asked firmly.

"I called your mother's house and there was no answer. I thought you said that you were helping your mom pack," he continued in a stiff tone of voice.

"My mom needed to go to grocery shopping, so I went with her."

"Oh......humph," he grunted. "I called you two hours ago. It took you two hours to go to the store?" He asked in an angry tone.

I swallowed hard and felt powerless.

"I, um, yeah. My mom likes to shop. We made a couple of other stops at other stores too," was the excuse I came up with.

I felt such resentment towards Jeremy, and I did not like him anymore, but I did not know how to tell him that.

What I really wanted to say was, "Jeremy, you are really an asshole, and your family is psychotic and the truth is I went out on a date with someone who treated me with respect."

But I didn't express and say how I truly felt. I was too afraid of my own truth. I was even more afraid of Jeremy and his Dr. Jekyll/Mr. Hyde psychotic rages.

I continued to sit on my bed and talk to Jeremy as the ice melted through the paper towel I had wrapped it in. I looked at the burn and wondered what my excuse would be when Jeremy asked me about it. Jeremy and I finished talking and he told me he was planning to come over. He hung up before I could say anything. I felt like I was swallowing quick sand; I did not want him to come over.

I got up off my bed and went to the bathroom to throw away the soggy paper towel. I glanced in the mirror at myself and just shook my head. Thoughts flooded my mind.

What was I doing with my life? I felt so confused, so misused, so misunderstood, and so very lost in a shuffle of negativity and did not know how to get myself out of this wreckage of my life.

I heard his truck pull into the driveway. I quickly freshened up my makeup and ran downstairs and faked a smile as Jeremy came in. Mom had walked away into the kitchen and left us. We kissed in greeting and I said, "Come on in."

Jeremy followed me as I stepped down into the den/family room.

"So, how is it going?" I asked him with a fake smile.

"Good," he said, looking me over. "What happened to your leg?" he continued.

I could not believe he noticed so quickly. I played dumb. "What?"

"Your leg- What happened to your leg?" he said accusingly.

I continued to play stupid and replied, "My leg?" "Oh, that!" I said as if I had just noticed the burn on my leg. "I um, was, um, curling my hair with Mom's hot iron and I dropped it.

"Humph," Jeremy grunted in disbelief.

"It looks like a motorcycle burn to me," he quickly snapped.

I looked at Jeremy trying to keep an innocent smile on my face. How could he have noticed my leg right away? Why would his first guess be a motorcycle burn? I wondered. Had he been stalking me and watching over my mom's house?

My stomach was all in knots as I stood there and continued to play stupid with a fake smile on my face.

I lived with the lie of telling Jeremy about the hot curling iron burn, as well as all the other stuff I held onto emotionally. As for Andy, he called my mom's house for at least three weeks, leaving messages for me to call him so we could get together again. I really liked Andy; he was genuine. Yet, I felt so stuck in this miserable relationship with Jeremy. I believed I was doomed if I even attempted a break up. My world was so very dark that I couldn't see even when I tried to.

I felt so small and powerless. I existed by crawling through this phase in my life and reaching out for anything and anyone I could grasp. Yet everything was so far out of reach. I was afraid to even look at the light at the end of the tunnel for fear of what others would think of me. I certainly did not think much of myself anymore.

The very last message Andy left on the answering machine was this,

"Hi Jinni, I really wish you would call me back. I really thought we shared something special on that first night we went out. I really would love to see you again. Please call me soon. I have been deported to Desert Storm; I leave the end of this week."

Every message he left pulled at my heart strings, yet I was stuck in my misery with a boyfriend I was afraid of. I never called Andy back. I think about Andy from time to time and wonder if he survived Desert Storm. The truth is that I will never know what became of Andy.

THE THREE OF LIFE
reminds me to think about;

1. **ATTITUDE** = When light is revealed un-expectantly, it is usually a sign from above to take a step back and re-evaluate life and the choices we have made for ourselves.

2. **LOVE** = Even though the smallest flicker of light is revealed in darkness, it can still be smothered by the dread of doubt.

3. **HEALTHY RELATIONSHIPS** = The only person that is able to wear us down is ourselves. We blame others for our failures and shortcomings, because we are unable to claim responsibility for our own actions and reactions.

"The Wise person questions himself, as the fool questions others."
~Henri Arnold, 1918

"Living life upside down you continue to reach for the stars only to realize at some point in time, that you are only grasping for what is beneath you."

~Anonymous

Chapter Six

For the Love of Pets

My mom and I did not communicate much about our lives. Our house was in final foreclosure stages and we had to move. I told her I was not going to be moving with her. We did not get along most of the time, as we did not see eye to eye on anything. My mom was happy to find herself a basement apartment in a town close by. She kept busy working for someone else's hair salon and dating this new boyfriend named Grant.

Dad, on the other hand, had broken up with Myrna and talked about possibly moving out of state to start his life over again. He frequently talked about moving to Arizona. I really did not believe he would move that far away, so it wasn't something we discussed when we spoke. I told my dad that Jeremy and I were looking for a place to move in to together. He did not respond to my news because he had been busy with his own life. He had raised my brother whom I did not see much of during the school years except at birthdays or holidays.

As I was so involved in my own life, I had pretty much alienated myself from my family except for holidays. I just kept my focus on feeling stuck and miserable in this world that I lived in. Jeremy and I had already established a consistently unstable relationship. We had been through so much together that we decided that we would rent a house and move in together. Why not? I figured. How much worse could it possibly get? I don't remember specific dates or sequence of events, yet, I can remember searching in the weekly newspaper for a house to rent. It wasn't long before I had found us a very cute, one bedroom house on a dead-end street in Hamptons, Long Island.

At the end of this street was a parking lot overlooking a scenic landscape around a lake. As I mentioned, this house was very cute. It was a ranch style house with a one car garage attached on the left and a laundry room attached to the back of the garage. There were stairs going down to a crawl space area which was actually an unfinished basement. The house sat on a quarter acre of property with no landscaping. It was painted white and you could tell it needed some TLC. Behind the house was a wooden deck/patio that extended out from the main bedroom. There was an orange tree that grew farther back in the yard where the neighbor's metal fence marked the boundary. There was another tree in the center of the backyard and another tree behind the laundry room.

The front door led into the living room/den and there was a closet directly across from the front door. To the left of this closet was the door that led into the garage. Beyond the living room to the right, was a medium sized kitchen that had a bathroom next to the refrigerator. If you continued to walk straight through the kitchen, you would walk into the dining room and then enter another door into the main bedroom. I don't recall the square footage of the home but it seemed to be just the right size. The house had hardwood floors throughout which were in desperate need of polishing.

Jeremy and I had agreed to rent from this landlord named David. We liked the house so much that we asked David if we could rent the house with a lease option to purchase.

David agreed and we signed the paperwork.

We moved in and fixed up the house. I had visited Home Depot several times to purchase plants and shrubbery to landscape the front yard. Jeremy and I had hired someone to come in and polish the wood floors and fix any broken pieces on the back wood deck. We visited a local city furniture store and ordered furniture to fill our home. We ordered a beautiful black, gold-trimmed entertainment unit and a fabric couch that was black with gold and blue tones throughout that looked as though someone had hand painted the wisps of gold and blue. It was very pretty and modern. The kitchen table and chairs matched the entertainment center.

The bedroom set was my original set from my mom's house which included an imitation Formica queen sized bed with head board and matching night stands, armoire and dresser.

We lived there together for two years. During this time we had gone to the animal shelter and adopted two Samoyed dogs. We named them "Nanook and Kayak". Over time, we realized that Kayak was more of a wolf breed because of his aggressive behavior. We found Kayak a dedicated owner that could handle him better then we could. We still had Nanook and not wanting him to be an only dog; we looked in the newspaper to adopt another dog.

NANOOK

That's when I found "Tramp," a pure breed Akita breed. Tramp's owner used her for breeding but because he did not want to use her anymore, he had posted in the newspaper, "AKITA, pure breed, free to good home". I remember going over to meet Tramp and her owner. She lived on a large piece of property that looked like a farm. There were chickens and dogs running everywhere. I took Tramp home and I believe we only kept her a week before we took her back to her original owner. She was very sweet, but she paced around the house nervously dripping blood from her rear end. We were more concerned about her health and thought it would be best if we took her back to her original owner. He told us that because she had had three litters already, she would frequently get her period. We felt we did not want to adopt a dog that had health issues so we left her with the owner. Looking back now, I know the right thing would have been to take her to my own vet and care for her myself. However, I cannot go back and only hope that she did have a good life.

TRAMP

I really didn't want Nanook to be an only dog so I went to the local pet store and fell in love with a tan and chocolate Chow-Chow puppy. I dragged Jeremy over and begged and pleaded to adopt /purchase this dog. We did indeed buy the puppy. We named him "Cookie" and he got along great with Nanook.

COOKIE

Chow-Chows are known to be aggressive dogs. Yet, Cookie was more docile than his reputation suggested. In addition to the dogs, I had also bought some lizards and frequently had to go to the pet store to buy them live crickets which was their recommended diet. I also had a fish tank that housed two mice. Of course, they quadrupled in time. Baby mice that were constantly being reproduced, I took them to the pet store to be sold; however, it wasn't long before I was told that the baby mice were used as breakfast for the snakes.

In the meantime, I had gotten a job in New York City, working as a secretary in the Garment district. I enjoyed the commute to work every day, traveling a total of three hours a day on the Long Island Railroad. I wasn't bothered by the travel time, it gave me time to just read or be still.

Over the two years of living with Jeremy, he frequently abused alcohol. Each time he got drunk, he called me every foul name one could think of and frequently punched holes in the walls. His biggest hobby was restoring a white 1979 Camaro that sat in our garage. Of course when he got drunk, his restorations didn't go just as expected. Then he threw temper tantrums which meant he threw things at the walls, hit me, or punched holes in the walls.

Jeremy threw his temper tantrums at night and when he was home on the weekends. Jeremy terrified me and the dogs were afraid of him too. Many nights, the three of us, Nanook, Cookie and me, hid in the bathroom on the floor with the lights off hoping he wouldn't find us and take out his anger on us. There were times that he came in the bathroom in a rage, flipped on the light switch and grabbed the dogs by their collars and threw them out of the bathroom sliding across the kitchen floor. Then he grabbed me by my hair and dragged me into the garage and told me he wanted to show me how things were not working out for him and his car.

I was so afraid of him. Though at the time I loved him, I hated him even more. I asked myself on many occasions: Why am I here? Why am I being treated this way? What have I done in my life to deserve this? I would frequently console myself and told myself that this relationship was not right. My body began to tell me so as well.

During my daily travels to New York City on the train I frequently read my Danielle Steel books. At this time in my life, my bottom lip began quivering like a nervous twitch. I had never had that before. The only reason I could give for it, was the stress that I lived with. I would tell myself, "Jinni, I don't know what a good relationship is, but this is not a good relationship. Sometimes I think we need to live and learn about what we don't want before we truly know what we want."

THE THREE OF LIFE
reminds me to think about;

1. **ATTITUDE** = Starting over is always a good change. Yet it's the attitude we keep that is most important as we move forward.

2. **LOVE** = Pets love unconditionally; they are our greatest teachers of love.

3. **Healthy Relationships** = The way we treat our pets at home is a tell tale sign of who we are and how we relate to our relationships. As for people, we unconsciously attract our own fear in reflections. When these reflections do not match the vibration in which we imagine ourselves to be, then is the time to make a shift in consciousness to strive for a better self.

"The dog trainer watched the dog chase his tail.
"Why do you chase your tail?" the dog trainer asked the dog.
"Because I was told that happiness is at the end of my tail", said the dog.
"Well then, if you just walk forward happiness will follow you" replied the dog trainer."
~Unknown

 A Holiday Hex

In the meantime, we were not able to make ends meet financially. I spent close to four hundred dollars a month on traveling expenses alone, which was half of my monthly paycheck. Therefore, I had been looking in the newspaper for a second job to work part time in the evenings.

I read about a telemarketing sales job that was a part time evening job from seven to eleven, three times a week and one Saturday a month. I figured this was perfect and as much as I hated telemarketing, I figured it would be an easy job. I called and scheduled an appointment to interview for this position. I recall meeting in a tall many-storied building in East Hampton. The office was a small room with eight chairs and desks that each held a telephone.

The company worked off cold-calling lists, and we were to call the people on the list and offer an extended warranty on hot water heaters. It was not my kind of favorite work, but I knew I could do it anyway. I got hired on the spot and started working the following week.

When I walked into the small, windowless office room, I realized immediately that I was the only woman there. Most of the men were in their thirties and forties; however, there was one man named Eric who was in his twenties. It made me feel a little better knowing I was not the youngest person in the room.

Eric and I got along very well, and as we got to know each other, we confided in each other about our personal lives. I complained about my unstable abusive relationship and most of the time he just listened. One night after work when it was pouring rain, Jeremy called me to tell me that he had to help his Dad with some repairs at their house and told me to get a ride home from someone. I told him I would get a ride somehow.

Jeremy and I had been sharing one car, a maroon Ford—F150 pick-up truck that we had recently purchased. That was the reason I asked Eric to drive me home. He did not hesitate to drive me home and told me that he was glad that I would not be driving home in this weather by myself.

The rain was really coming down and I was glad I was not driving. The roads were slippery and not safe to drive on in nasty weather. I gave him directions to my house and practically yelled as the rain pitter pattered on the roof of the car. We pulled into my drive way and he turned off the car.

"My boyfriend is not home; he is at his parents' house helping them with some house repairs," I yelled as the sound of the rain drowned my voice. Eric smiled.

"Why don't you come in for a few minutes until the rain lets up? It is really not good weather for anyone to be driving in," I said concerned. Eric smiled and nodded in agreement. I got out of the car and ran to the front door with Eric following me. My dogs greeted me at the door.

"Hi Nanook and Cookie," I said cheerfully.

"Say hello to Eric," I continued to say to my dogs.

"Hey guys!" Eric said joyfully. "This is a nice place you have here Jinni." Eric said as he stood in the entrance way and looked around. "I should probably get going as soon as the rain lets up. I would hate for your boyfriend to come home and find me here."

"Yeah, he would probably kill you," I said half-jokingly. "Go ahead and have a seat on the couch; you might as well make yourself comfortable and watch some television until the rain lets up," I continued.

"Actually, I would rather just sit here and talk to you." Eric said in a matter of fact tone.

"Um, ok," I said nervously as my stomach tightened up. "I just need to get myself something to drink. Would you like some soda?" I asked hospitably. Eric looked at me and nodded his head 'no.' I left the room and went into the kitchen. When I returned, Eric was sitting on the couch petting Nanook, who sat in front of him while Cookie lay on the carpet to the right of him.

"I see you have made some new friends," I said with a smile.

"Yep I sure did," Eric replied with a smile. Eric had been looking at Nanook when I had re-entered the room, but now he was looking at me.

"Well, it sure is pouring outside. Are you sure it's ok that I am here?" Eric said concerned. I looked at him, as my stomach was tangled in knots, and I knew very well that Jeremy would not only kill him, but he would beat the you-know-what out of me if he only knew that I let another man in the house. Yet, I did not listen to my feelings and I said, "Of course it's ok. I faked a smile and continued,

"This weather is not safe to drive in. As soon as it lets up you can leave."

"Well, then why don't you sit with me and we can talk?"

"Ok," I responded nervously. I sat down on the couch next to Eric and we talked about work and about the college classes he was taking to become a massage therapist. I smiled and told him that I was happy that he was going to school and focusing on what he wanted to do. The conversation got quiet and the energy in the room became awkward.

"How about I give you a back massage? It would ease some of your tension," he suggested.

"Oh...um....ok." I only wish he knew how tense I felt.

"Just lay down here on the couch and I will give you a massage."

I felt stuck. I did not know what to do other than to lie down on the couch as he preceded to give me a back massage. All I could think about was Jeremy walking through the front door at any time.

Eric had been massaging my back for about ten minutes when the telephone rang. I got up and told Eric I would be right back.

I went into the kitchen, leaping for the phone before it rang too many times "Hello?" I said.

"What took you so long to answer the phone?" Jeremy's voice growled.

"I um, I was in the other room. Sorry. When are you coming home?" I trembled in my response.

"I should be home by nine-thirty or ten." I looked at the clock on the wall that said eight thirty as I listened to him continue, "I am still helping my dad repair some of the plumbing underneath the kitchen sink for my mom. We need to get this done so she doesn't flip out and have to do the dishes in the bathroom sink," he continued.

"Oh, ok. Well, I will see you when you get home," I stated, trying to rush off the phone.

"Yeah, see you then," Jeremy hung up the phone first.

I hung up the phone and hurried back into the television room.

"Hi, sorry about that. My boyfriend should be home within an hour or so."

"Ok, well, good. That's just enough time. Come back here and lay down so I can finish giving you a massage," Eric said motioning me back to the couch. I smiled, as I was uncertain about his intentions. I walked back to the couch and lay down on my stomach.

Eric began to massage my back again and this time, his hands began to roam upon my butt and then in between my legs. I lifted my head up and said,

"Eric, this is really not a good idea."

"Shhhhh", he said as he leaned closer to me and began to kiss my right ear,

"It's ok, your boyfriend won't be home for a while," he whispered in my ear as he continued to kiss my ear and behind my ear and down my neck. His hands began to roam from my back motioning me to turn over. From there, he proceeded to fondle my breasts. He leaned forward again and began to kiss me. Before I knew it, we had our clothes off and he had inserted himself inside of me. After he came, he became very jittery as he put on his clothes quickly and told me he had to leave. It was nine o'clock and the rain had let up some.

As he left, he apologized for his behavior yet told me he would see me at work tomorrow. About ten minutes after Eric left, I took the dogs outside as the truck pulled into our drive way. Jeremy was home.

I faked a smile as I stood there watching him get out of the truck. I swallowed a lump of guilt, shame and disgust. As Jeremy got out of the truck, he looked at me and mimicked Jack Nicholson's character and tone of voice from the movie, 'The Shining', with an evil expression on his face he said, "Honey, I'm home."

I did not tell Jeremy anything about Eric bringing me home and he didn't ask.

The next day I spent the whole day contemplating whether or not I wanted to continue working at my night job. The thought of seeing Eric after last night, was going to seem awkward. Was I a victim of rape in my own home? Why was I so naïve to let him into my house? He seemed like a nice guy. I don't understand why I continue to be victimized. Is it against the human code to be graceful and hospitable?

The day flew by and before I knew it, I had to get myself ready for my night job. I swallowed my shame as I got in my car and arrived early. The door was locked, and I sat outside the door waiting for someone to get there. My boss, Leroy, eventually showed up. Leroy was an obese white man with very thin stringy, greasy hair that he parted to the side to make it look like he had more hair. He wore very thick, large-rimmed glasses that just made his face look larger. He always dressed in a plaid button down shirt and the same color tan slacks. I wondered if they were the only pants he had that fit him.

"Waiting long?" he said calmly.

"Not too long." I stated with a smile. Leroy unlocked the door and I followed him inside.

"Jinni, we have to talk," he said sternly.

"Oh. Ok," I replied having no idea why we had to talk.

"Jinni I did not get a chance to call you today, but I figured we could talk in person tonight. I called the other guys and told them to take the night off." I continued to sit there quietly and shake my head in a yes gesture as I kept a smile on my face and listened.

"Jinni, we are going to have to let you go. You are not keeping up with sales, and it just doesn't pay to have you here," he said bluntly.

I had not expected this at all. I continued to shake my head in agreement and said,

"Oh, ok, um..........sorry."

Leroy smiled and looked at the door, motioning with his head for me to leave.

"We will mail you your paycheck."

I got up from my seat feeling a bit robotic and numb. I hadn't expected this at all. I knew my sales were down. In fact, I hated doing cold calls. I hated doing any kind of sales work. I walked back to my car and drove home.

"What am I going to tell Jeremy?" I thought. He is going to think I am such a failure for losing my part time job. I feared going home.

When I got home, I could see the lights on in the garage. I sat in my car for a few minutes in contemplation before getting out and going in the house. I dreaded having to deal with Jeremy.

I walked into the house to be greeted by the dogs and to hear Jeremy screaming in the garage about how he messed up on his car. Then I could hear him punch a hole in the wall. I swallowed what felt like a boulder as I walked to the garage door. I opened the door and peeked in. He looked at me and screamed, "What the fuck are you doing home?"

I ignored Jeremy as I about faced and went into the bathroom to wash up. I had hoped that Jeremy would calm down and I would eventually tell him I lost my part time job. He did eventually calm down and I did tell him that I did not do well enough on the sales and they had to let me go. He responded with a chuckle by saying,

"I am not surprised you lost the job, there is not much you're good at anyway."

It was two weeks before Christmas. As much as I hated the job, I was still feeling a little disappointed to have lost it because we could have used the extra money.

Jeremy told me that his boss was throwing a Christmas party the following Friday night. He told me it was going to be held at his work place. In the garage shop where engines for automobiles were rebuilt.

The night of the party, we saw how his boss tried to make an auto body repair shop seem festive, as he had used green plastic table cloths to cover three folding tables which were lined up against the lobby entrance wall. Each table was filled with an array of goodies. On the first table, there was the alcohol, sodas, an ice pitcher and plastic cups. There was a cooler filled with beer that sat on the right side of the table. The second table held festive paper plates, napkins and plastic utensils and large portions of potato salad and cole slaw containers. The eye catcher on this table was a six-foot hero (hoagie) that spread out across the table. The third table had three hot trays, each with a different choice of food; there was lasagna, chicken cutlets, and sausage with peppers.

There was one small folding table with a red plastic table cloth that sat across from the three large folding tables which held a tray of cookies. The food had been catered by a local Italian restaurant, a favorite of Jeremy's boss.

Jeremy worked with three guys: his boss Rick, and two co-workers, Jeff and Sal. Rick was a short guy with black hair and a black beard. His wife, who accompanied him, was just as petite. She had long black hair and a pretty Barbie doll face, yet she wore a lot of makeup. Rick was a nice guy and always appeared to have a smile on his face. His wife appeared to be humbly pleasant.

Jeff was a tall thin guy with grey spiked hair and a grey scruffy face. Jeff reminded me of the character, Shaggy from Scooby Doo. He was just a bit older and greyer. He was with his girlfriend Jane. Jane was a bit rough looking. She was tall and thin. She had long, bleached out blonde straggly dry hair and could have used some makeup. She seemed nice too, but she liked to smoke a lot.

Sal, in contrast to Jeff, was a heavy set man with black curly hair and a thick black mustache. He reminded me of, Mario from the Mario Brothers arcade game. His wife was a bit on the chunky side too. She had long brown curly hair and wore ruby red lipstick. She had a funny sense of humor and was very outgoing. She dressed in tight blue jeans and a red sweater.

It seemed to be a nice party. Of course, everyone began to drink before they ate. The more people drank, the easier it was to talk to each other and it lightened the atmosphere and added cheer for the holidays. I had a rum and coke before I began to eat. As the night went on, I eventually had my portion of food. After everyone else had eaten too, the guys felt it was time to do tequila shots. Alcohol puts me to sleep, so one or two drinks do me in.

I did not want to do shots; yet, everyone else was doing shots and they were cheering me on to do a shot. I don't remember how many shots I did, and I really don't remember how I ended up where I found myself to be next.

I had awakened to what I thought to be Jeremy's hand down my unzipped jeans into my underpants. He was kissing and sticking his tongue into my left ear as I lay on my right side across the front seat of a truck. I began to moan as his hand had been stroking my vagina and as he kept inserting one of his fingers into my vagina.

I began to cry out, "Oh, Jeremy."

"It's not Jeremy," the male voice said.

I immediately sat up to look and see who this man was.

"Shhhh, its ok Jinni. It's me Sal," he said as he took his hand out from my underpants and whispered as he leaned over to kiss me on the lips.

I pulled away and stated in disgust, "What are you doing? Why are you here? Why am I here? Where is Jeremy and where is your wife?!"

"You looked like you were going to pass out so I picked you up and carried you to my truck. I turned on the truck and put on the heat for you because it is cold outside. I figured you could seep off some of the alcohol. Yet, when I saw you lying there, I just couldn't resist. Jeremy is inside. He wasn't paying any attention to you. I have always admired you and wanted you. Oh Jinni, I want you so bad." he moaned.

I not only felt disgusted, I also felt like I was stuck in a nightmare. How was this happening? I couldn't grasp my reality.

"Where is Jeremy and isn't your wife inside?" I asked feeling confused.

"Yeah, she is inside, but she doesn't care what I do. Oh Jinni," Sal began to moan as he leaned towards me again and began to kiss my face and forcefully stick his tongue in my mouth. I kept trying to pull away but his grasp around my arms was so very tight. Then the driver's side door opened.

"What's going on here?" It was Jeremy. "Ah nothing. I was just checking on your girl here. Just making sure it's nice and warm in here for her," Sal said acting innocent as he got out of the driver's side of the truck.

"Let's go Jinni! This is not our truck!" Jeremy spoke in a firm threatening voice.

I looked at him and then opened the passenger door. I buttoned my jeans as I got myself out of the truck.

"Let's go. I am taking you home!" Jeremy said in an angry tone. We walked over to our truck and got in. Jeremy started up the truck.

"We have to wait a few minutes for the truck to warm up. So, did you have fun?"

Jeremy continued in a threatening voice. I did not say a word.

"Answer me you slut!!" he continued. "So, you're messing around with Sal? I see how you are."

I tried to explain that I had no idea how I got into Sal's truck. Jeremy did not believe a word I said. As I continued to tell him that I didn't even remember ever leaving the party or passing out or getting into Sal's truck, Jeremy did not want to hear me.

Instead, he yelled, "Shut up you slut!"

I cried like a baby. I did not say a word, yet my inner dialog agreed with him.

"Yeah, I am a slut, I am disgusting," I repeated in my head. "All that guys want from me is to have sex. I am nothing more than this to anyone." "But you are more," an inner voice said, "You deserve better than this." I didn't know what was right, but I knew that my teenage years had been wrecked and my early adult life was so wrong. I was very stuck. I didn't know how to get out of that dark merry-go-round of a world."

My inner dialog eventually quieted down when we pulled into our driveway at home. Jeremy got out and slammed the truck door. I sat motionless. I eventually got out of the truck went inside and washed up for bed. Jeremy and I did not talk.

The next day, Jeremy received a call from his best friend, Scotty. Jeremy hung up the phone after talking with Scotty and approached me.

"Scotty wants to invite us over tonight for a little Christmas celebration."

"Oh, ok," I responded. I really did not like Scotty that much; he was just large and slimy looking. Scotty was an obese twenty-seven year old that had more hair on his face than I had ever seen on anyone. He lived in a basement apartment with his girlfriend Laura.

We drove over to Scotties place that evening. We walked to the side of the house and down the stairs to the apartment. Jeremy knocked on the door and Scotty answered in seconds.

"Hey guys! Come on in!"

We walked into what was a combined small kitchen/den area with lots of alcohol and a bowl of chips on the yellow table cloth.

"All….right! Hey Laura, call Dominos and order us a couple of pizzas," Scotty called to her.

We followed Scotty and sat down on the worn out couch. I was kind of disgusted and did not want to sit down, but I did not want to be rude.

"So how ya guys doing?" Scotty began. We both smiled as we looked at him.

There was a knock at the door. "Pizza already!?" Scotty said a little confused.

He got up and opened the door.

"Ah, hey there Rocky! Come on in."

I could not see at first who he was talking too. Then it was more than obvious because he stood there holding a fifteen pound raccoon.

Jeremy and I looked at each other and laughed nervously.

"Rocky, meet Jinni and Jeremy," Scotty said as he brought Rocky in to feed him.

"Yeah, me an Laura have been feeding this little guy, and now he visits us every day by knocking on the door." Scotty continued.

I love animals, but I thought raccoons were dangerous. Then I got to pet Rocky and he seemed harmless.

Scotty let Rocky back outside as the pizza man arrived with our Domino's pizza. The guys had already begun to drink beers and Laura and I had begun drinking wine coolers.

We shared some laughs and pizza and chips and just talked about nothing important. Then Scotty said, almost whispering, "Hey I got a good video for us to watch." I wasn't feeling very comfortable at all now.

Then Scotty began to talk about the playboy channel and he pulled out playboy books which Jeremy, he and Laura were drooling over. I felt so uncomfortable and just wanted to go home. Then Scotty turned on the television and played the VHS that he had sitting on top of the television.

Scotty sat on a large lazy boy chair as Laura sat on his lap facing the television. I had not moved and was still sitting next to Jeremy. We watched this raunchy pornographic movie that showed two girls making out and then a girl and a guy fooling around.

Out of the blue, Jeremy said, "Ooooh yeah see how she is doing that? My ex- girlfriend Lana used to do that to me. That's what I like."

Scotty laughed as Jeremy went on about what his ex-girlfriend used to do to him. I looked at Jeremy and said, "Do you not see me sitting here?"

He chuckled in response, "You don't take care of me the way Lana used to take care of me." He remarked.

And with that I took my half empty wine cooler and poured it in his lap.

"You are such a pig," I said. "Just take me home. I don't want to be here watching this trash." I continued in a tone of disgust.

Scotty and Laura were hysterically laughing while I sat there with a frown on my face. I just wanted to cry, I felt so disrespected. To make the situation worse, Scotty and Laura thought my reaction was the funniest thing ever. I felt like I was not appreciated at all.

Jeremy and I eventually left and drove home in silence.

Then I broke the silence. "Are you still seeing Lana?" I asked.

"No!" Jeremy replied immediately.

"Oh," I stated without effort as I continued, "I was just wondering because I was cleaning out the laundry room last week and I found a shoe box with a brand new pair of very nice tall, black boots, and this morning, while I was folding laundry, I noticed that the box was gone."

Silence filled the truck so thick that you could cut it with a knife.

"Oh, that. I was going to give them to you for Christmas but I changed my mind and decided to return them," Jeremy replied in a cold flat tone.

I sat in silence gripped by an ice-cold feeling of disbelief. We drove home the rest of the way in the same silence.

Before we went to sleep, the tension in the air was so very thick, but out of nowhere Jeremy said, "Let's get married."

It was an eighty degree turn from where we had been all evening. I was surprised and elated, as any girl would be, when her boyfriend asks her to get married.

"Ok!" I immediately responded with a huge smile on my face, forgetting all about the evening's events. My emotions were so tossed, yet, I played along.

"Well, I don't have a ring to give you and I don't have a lot of money to buy a fancy ring.

Maybe you can go to the consignment shop this week and pick yourself up a ring."

"Ok, sure. I can do that. In fact maybe we can go together tomorrow?" I asked.

"Yeah, we'll see tomorrow," Jeremy said coldly.

The next morning came and I awoke cheerful and excited to pick out an engagement ring. It was Sunday and I knew that the consignments shop would be open by noon.

"Let's go out shopping. We can stop at the grocery store and then we can go by the consignment shop together to pick out that ring," I said joyfully.

"Nah. I got stuff to do around the house here. You don't need me to go shopping and you can pick out the ring yourself," he said discouragingly.

"Oh, Ok," I responded disappointed. I washed, dressed and was ready to go. I got into my car and went straight to the consignment shop first.

Two very tall men stood behind the glass showcase that sat in the middle of the room.

"Hi young lady, can we help you?" One of the men said.

"Ah, yes, I am looking for an engagement ring," I said.

"Oh, ok. We have some right here in this section." The man walked two steps and unlocked the back door of the showcase window.

"And who is this for? Is this for you?" he asked in a deep voice.

"Ah, yes, this is for me. I am picking out my own engagement ring." I smiled as I said this, but my stomach turned upside down as I thought to myself, "This is not how it's supposed to be. The guy is the one who picks out the ring."

I continued to smile; however, and peered in the glass showcase that held the rings. I pointed to a silver ring with a square-cut diamond in the center. "I like that one. I would like to see that one," I said. He handed the ring to me. I stared at it for a moment or two. It appeared to be an antique style ring and I thought it was very unique.

"What's the story on this ring and how much is it?" I asked.

"This is an antique ring that has only been worn by princesses and queens. We are asking twenty nine dollars for it. But today, we will offer you a special price of twelve dollars," he said firmly.

"Um....ok, Wow! Princesses and queens, huh? There must be some history attached to this ring!" I said with a smile. "Ok, I will take it." I handed him the twelve dollars and he put the ring in a ring box and wrote me a receipt. He put the receipt and the ring box in a small paper sandwich bag and handed it to me.

"Thank you," I said with a smile.

"You bet. Good luck to you," he said as I walked out the door. I put the bag in my purse and instead of heading to the grocery store, I went home. When I walked in the front door, Jeremy was sitting on the couch drinking a beer.

Nanook and Cookie were sitting on either side of him on the wood floors. He looked at me and smiled, lifted his beer up toward me and said, "I figured this would take care of the hangover. I hope you bought more beer at the store because this is the last one in the fridge."

"I…um, haven't gone to the store yet," I said feeling terribly guilty.

Jeremy's face turned from a smile to a frown, and his tone changed from friendly to angry as he responded, "What do you mean you haven't gone to the store yet?

Where have you been, you bitch!"

"I…um, um, went to the consignment shop and I was so excited to have found a ring that I wanted to come home first to show it to you before I go grocery shopping," I swallowed hard. Jeremy put his legs up on the coffee table and crossed them.

"Yeah, ok, I will take a look," he said belligerently. I was shaking with fear, yet, I tried not to show it. I pulled the bag out of my purse and handed it to him. He looked at the bag and then he looked at me.

"Open it!" he said in an almost defiant tone. I opened the small bag, and removed the ring-box. I handed him the box and he just stared at it. After a couple of seconds, I realized he was not going to take it and open it so I opened the ring box and held it in front of his face.

"What do you think?" I asked with a smile.

"Yeah, it's nice. You can go get me some beer now," he said as a statement not as a question. I felt neglected. "Um, ok. Um, what about the ring? Do you want me to wrap it? Do you want to give it to me, maybe ask me in an official way to marry you?" I said bewildered.

There was silence for a second or two, "Huh? I wonder what time the races start today." He got up, opened the entertainment center, grabbed the remote control from off of the television and went to sit back on the couch almost as if I weren't even there. Once he sat back down, he looked at me and paused for a moment after turning the television on, "Oh, yeah, well if you like the ring. I already asked ya so just wear the ring," he said coldly.

That really was not the answer I was hoping to hear. None of this was happening like the story books told me. I did not like how my life had been unfolding. Despite how I felt, I took the ring out of the box and placed it on my ring finger.

"Ok, I am going to go to the grocery store now." Jeremy was watching the television and acted as if he did not hear me. So I walked out the front door, got into my car and headed to the grocery store.

"This is really messed up." I said to myself out loud. "This is not how I had imagined my life to be. He doesn't care about me. All he cares about is his beers and his car."

I drove nodding my head in disagreement. "Jinni what are you doing?"

I continued to mumble to myself. I got to the store and once I went inside and began shopping, the voices in my head stopped chattering.

THE THREE OF LIFE
reminds me to think about;

1. **ATTITUDE** = You are taken advantage of and victimized only if you allow it to be so. One must learn posture.

2. **LOVE** = Posture is perhaps the most obvious non verbal signal of self-confidence and belief in yourself. Adopting the behavior of confidence-the posture, the actions, and the thoughts-starts you on the upward spiral of increasing self-confidence.

3. **HEALTHY RELATIONSHIPS** = It is wise to become influential and not always easily influenced. Inspiration comes from healthy support from healthy relationships. On the contrary, when our relationships are not supporting yet discouraging, it is necessary to eliminate those relationships for our own health.

"Good judgment comes from experience, and experience comes from bad judgment."

~Barry LePatner

"There is no use trying to change
another person who annoys you.
However, you can change your
reaction to that person so that
his or her behavior doesn't matter
so much to you.
Your reaction is
what affects YOU, not the other
person's behavior. When you react
to a situation in a non-
judgmental way, you will diffuse
the situation."

~Anonymous

Chapter Eight

Enough is Enough

I talked to my dad every couple of weeks. When I spoke with him again, he told me that he had met another lady friend named Rachel. He expressed that he really liked Rachel and I knew for certain that he wouldn't move out of state now. To my surprise; however, he told his girlfriend that he planned to move to a place where he did not know anyone.

He specifically mentioned Arizona with its mountains and fresh air and the spirit of freedom. He did move and shortly after his move, Rachel put her house up for sale and planned to fly to Arizona and move in with my dad once her house sold.

In the meantime, Rachel still lived with two of her three older kids; Gina, Bobby and Jenna. Bobby had gotten married and had moved out and Gina was engaged to be married and Jenna was finishing high school.

So, at age twenty-two after my parents had been divorced for 6 years, my father moved to Arizona with his girlfriend pending her move and my mother moved to Florida with her boyfriend. There was also my very beloved brother, Ezra, who decided to move in with my dad to attend college in Arizona. So, there I was living on my own, actually living with Jeremy at the time. I kept in touch with both my parents despite the fact that I had felt neglected and abandoned by them. I was angry with them for moving so far away. Both my parents had separately invited me to come live with them, yet I hadn't wanted to leave my friends or my boyfriend.

The landlord that Jeremy and I had been renting from came to visit us for the renewal or our lease. We had really fixed up the place since the last time he had been there and he was really impressed with what we had done. We told him that we wanted to purchase the house and property. He told us that he changed his mind and did not want to sell it after all. This was discouraging.

It was springtime and I began to see flying bugs in our home in various places. One day when I came home from work, the house was swarming with these flying bugs. I called the landlord who called an exterminator. The exterminator came the next day. Having to spend the night in the house with those flying bugs freaked me out. I did not sleep well at all.

I called into work to tell them that I had to stay home to deal with some issues. Jeremy left to go to work and I was home waiting for the exterminator. When he arrived, he walked in the house, smiled and stated, "Oh, I see you have a termite infestation." I grinned in response. He said he was going to fumigate the house but first had to find where the nest was. He spent some time walking around the house, garage and laundry room. Then he crawled into the unfinished basement.

When he returned he said in a jolly matter of fact tone of voice,

"Well, I found your nest! It's in the unfinished basement. In fact, this entire house should be bull dozed because the termites have infested all the walls of the house."

I grinned in response.

He fumigated the house the best he could and then I called the landlord to tell him what the exterminator said. The landlord didn't seem to be moved by the news of the infestation. I mean, why would he? He wasn't living in the house. I unwillingly called Jeremy to tell him the news. His response was a repetitive, "Humph."

When Jeremy and I were talking again, we decided we were going to move to another house. I went house hunting and found a beautiful, colonial style house on a corner lot.

Upon entering the house, I noticed the family room with hard wood floors. Beyond this room I saw the open kitchen. To the right was a hallway which led to three bedrooms.

Half of the house had been reconstructed as a one bedroom apartment that could be rented out. There was a full basement and the house stood on half an acre of property.

Best of all, the house appeared to be bug free.

I really liked the house and thought it was a great investment, especially with the added apartment that would help pay our mortgage. We had the realtors and financiers work with us on getting a mortgage for the house. We went through several different banks, each one denying us a mortgage.

Then it happened. It was a beautiful, warm and sunny Saturday and I had an early Saturday morning doctor appointment for a routine check-up and I received a clean bill of health. I returned home and called out to Jeremy,

"Hi Jeremy, I am home." There was no answer.

I looked around the inside of the house, then in the garage. I didn't see him anywhere. Then I went back through the bedroom and found Jeremy sitting on a chair on the back deck.

"Hi," I said with a smile. He looked at me with a blank stare.

"Did you get me some sunscreen?" he said on the verge of throwing a fit. I was confused by the question.

"Huh? Sunscreen? I had a doctor's appointment; I didn't go to the store. I did not know that you needed sunscreen," I stated innocently.

With that Jeremy got up and screamed and spit in my face as he yelled, "I need sunscreen! How am I supposed to mow the lawn and not get sunburned? I need sunscreen!"

I looked at him trembling and said softly the boldest thing I ever said to him,

"Well, you know where the store is; you can go get yourself some sunscreen."

I grimaced and turned to walk back inside. All of a sudden he grabbed my long hair as I screamed. He threw me across the patio deck. I fell down and looked up at him. He grabbed me again and yelled, "You selfish bitch! I need sunscreen!"

I crawled my way back inside through the bedroom door. He sat there and watched me.

As I passed him he kicked me and laughed. I got into the house and stood up.

I went to the bathroom as the dogs followed me and locked the bathroom door. It was quiet for a few minutes. Then I was startled by the pounding on the bathroom door.

It was Jeremy, "Open the door!" He yelled in a threatening voice. I was so afraid I wedged myself under the sink to hide from him. I did not get up to open the door. He kicked the door open and grabbed me by my hair and dragged me out of the bathroom into the kitchen.

"What is wrong with you?" he yelled.

Before I could even breathe, I felt the side of his hand land a karate chop to the back of my neck. I nearly blacked out as I collapsed. I couldn't feel my body at first. As I regained consciousness, I heard the rumbling of the truck engine outside. I stood up and cried, "I can't do this anymore."

When Jeremy came back from wherever he went, we did not talk. On Sunday, we ignored each other.

Monday morning arrived, and after Jeremy left for work as usual, I called into work and told them that I was not feeling well and I would not be coming into work. At nine o'clock, I called Rachel, whom had been packing up her house, as well as getting ready for Gina's wedding and then her move to Arizona. Through tears, I literally begged her to help me. I told her what happened, leaving out specific details, but I told her enough that she understood that I needed to leave before he killed me. She agreed to pick me up and offered to let me stay with her until I was able to find my own place to live. The only down side to her kind offer was that I was going to have to leave my dogs. I truly did not want to leave them behind; yet, I knew that I had to save myself. I hoped I could come back for them another time. Yet, deep in my mind I knew that I never wanted to come back to this house.

I asked Rachel to pick me up around three o'clock. That would give me plenty of time to pack what I could take. I packed in a hurry: my clothes, my makeup and toiletries, my jewelry, and my twelve hundred dollar Kirby vacuum cleaner. That was it. I dreaded leaving the dogs, the furniture, the kitchen cook ware and accessories, but I had no other choice.

I ripped a piece of paper from the notepad that was on the refrigerator, grabbed a pen from out of the junk drawer, and stood at the kitchen island as I began to write a note to Jeremy:

Dear Jeremy,

I am sorry, but I cannot live this way anymore and I must leave you. We have talked numerous times about your drinking and your wavering character. I have tried to encourage you to seek help with Alcoholics Anonymous or even counseling; yet, you choose for things to stay the same.

Please do not try to find me. When I can, I will try and come back for the dogs.

Love, Jinni

PS: I canceled your car insurance so you will need to get your own.

When we got back to Rachel's house, we put all my stuff in the garage. I had dinner with Rachel and her kids. Gina was excited over her wedding which was to be in the next two weeks and we talked about her visions of her wedding day. She invited me to go shopping with her after dinner, to pick up some accessories for her wedding dress. My head was pounding and I felt so drained that I had to decline the invitation.

Rachel had told me that I could sleep on the couch since all the other beds were taken. I felt safe and I didn't care where I slept. Gina came back around eight thirty in the evening crying.

"What's the matter Gina?" Rachel yelled with sincerity from her bedroom.

Through hysterical tears, Gina sobbed out, "I can't find matching underwear for my wedding dress."

I heard Rachel hold back a chuckle as she replied, "Gina we will go shopping again tomorrow and I promise you we will find matching underwear."

Although I had been grieving over my day, this little exchange made me smile.

It was around nine thirty and everyone was still awake but getting ready to go to sleep. I lay on the couch and stared at the ceiling as tears rolled down the sides of my face into my hair. I was thinking about my life and my day. I couldn't believe that I left. I wasn't sure which emotion was stronger, the feeling of safety or the fear of what Jeremy would do if he found me.

Rachel's phone rang and my heart jumped. Rachel called down from her room, "Jinni, Jeremy is on the phone."

I hesitated and unwillingly answered the phone on the end table, "Hello," I said fearing the worst.

"So you're at Rachel's huh? I'm coming over; we need to talk about this."

"Jeremy, if you dare come to this house or even step foot on this property, I will call the police!" Rachel interrupted from the other line.

She obviously had not hung up her extension.

"I just want to talk to Jinni, Rachel."

"I think you have done enough damage. You are not to talk to Jinni and DO NOT come to my house. If you dare to show up here, I will not hesitate to call the cops."

"But, Jinni, I love you," Jeremy pleaded.

Rachel continued to listen on the other line while I said sympathetically, "Jeremy, you really need to go for counseling. You are an alcoholic. I tried to work this out with you and I suggested counseling on various occasions but you deny that you have a problem with alcohol."

"Ok, I will go for help," Jeremy replied.

"I have to go now," I said as I hung up the phone. I was devastated and broke down in tears. I felt so bad for him.

I lived with Rachel for two weeks. During those two weeks, I received a phone call from Jeremy's mother.

"Hello Jinni, this is Anita. Jeremy is threatening to commit suicide if you don't go back to him," she said in her stern French accent.

"Hi Mrs. Moreau, I'm sorry to hear that, but I cannot go back to Jeremy. He needs to go for therapy to help him learn to control his drinking and his temper," I said sternly.

I was so scared on the inside. I feared this woman with every thread of my being.

"Oh. Well, if you don't go back to him he will kill himself!" she said again in that stern matter of fact tone.

"I'm sorry. I cannot be with him anymore. I have to go now. Goodbye."

I hung up the phone and took a deep breath. I was proud of myself for not caving in and for sticking up for myself.

I never went back to rescue my dogs. I have lived with regret for many years over that, but I knew I could not take care of them. I hope they had a good life after I left. Over the past few years I have tried to locate Cookie through an implanted microchip that was in my name and I learned he had been adopted by another family. As for Nanook, I can only guess that Jeremy kept him.

THE THREE OF LIFE
reminds me to think about:

1. **ATTITUDE** = When our perception and vision of reality is not clear, we fear what we already know.

2. **LOVE** = Self confidence raises the bar on loving ourselves first.

3. **HEALTHY RELATIONSHIPS** = Many times we can't find a solution because we focus more on the problem. For every problem, there is a SOLUTION. The frustration is that sometimes we are so close to the problem, that we can't see the SOLUTION! Stepping back and re evaluating the problem at hand helps us to realign ourselves and our boundaries.

"What probably distorts everything in life is that one is convinced that one is speaking the truth because one says what one thinks."
~ SACHA GUITRY, 1885-1959

"Self—respect is the root of discipline: The sense of Dignity grows with the ability to say no to oneself."
~ Abraham Joshua Heschel, 1907-1915

To wish you could have just made a better choice in the past is really pointless because you have a clean slate every second from which you can make a better choice and to start anew NOW.
—THE DAILY GURU

Chapter Nine

The Cat Crack House

One month later, I was living downstairs in the same apartment as my grandmother Agnes, in Flushing Queens. It felt good to live near my grandmother who was a typical short and stocky Italian older woman with a heavy Italian accent. She did not like being alone much and with me living downstairs we were able to get together every now and then to play the Italian card game called 'Scupa." I don't recall how to play but I think we were supposed to match the cards we had in our hand with cards that we picked up.

While living downstairs from my grandmother I had adopted three cats whom I had named Mickey, Mini and Pluto. Mickey was a typical orange cat. He was so funny and easy-going; he would lie on his back while I used the mini dust buster to vacuum his belly. Pluto was a black and white cat who was a bit of a straight character and then there was Mini, a calico, who was very pretty and very sassy.

I loved these cats. They were very entertaining. One day Pluto got out the front door of my apartment through the front door. I was devastated and looked for him, yet being in a city near the train station and not far from the expressway, I doubted I would ever see him again. To my surprise a week later when I was returning home from my long day in the city, guess who showed up at the front door. Pluto! Not only was it Pluto, but he brought another cat friend with him. When I knelt down to pick up Pluto, the other cat ran away. I was so happy Pluto was home. I was still working in New York City in the garment district as a secretary. My grandmother's apartment building was around the corner from the Long Island Railroad. It was convenient and I loved the everyday commute into the city. I always met lots of people on the train. Sometimes the same people sat with me and sometimes there was an entire new group of people.

One day on my train ride home, a gentleman sitting in the row next to mine wondered if I was interested in meeting his brother and asked me for my number. I had been single for a month now and was flattered that I was asked to be set up with someone's brother.

I gave the man my number and the next day I received a call from Kenny. He introduced himself and we talked for a while on the phone. I recall he was very funny and we made plans to have dinner that coming weekend. I was fearlessly naïve and thought it would be ok if he just came to my place to pick me up. The day came and he picked me up at my apartment. We went to a local Italian restaurant and I recall laughing a lot and really enjoying his company. He had lots of jokes to tell and we just really hit it off.

After that I began a new job selling rare coins for Dalton Coin Company. I had made some new friends, or so I thought and confided to them about my new boyfriend's constant abuse with pot and partying. They had discouraged me from continuing to see my boyfriend and set me up with another guy by the name of Parker who was a friend of theirs who worked in the same coin company that had recently hired me.

The new friends felt we would be a perfect match though they knew very little about me. After a month or so of dating, Parker told me that he loved me and that he wanted to take care of me and that I should move into his house with him. I thought it was a fun idea and agreed to move in with him.

I went back home and talked to my grandmother who was disappointed to hear that I was going to move. I had been paying my grandmother month to month for the rent so I stayed another two weeks in hopes that she could find another tenant.

I packed up my things to move again and was very excited to be moving in with my new boyfriend who seemed to promise so much. A week or so before the move, I had called Parker and asked him if it was okay to bring the cat litter box and the cats over before I moved all the furniture and big stuff.

"Cats? You can't bring the cats here," he stated clearly.

"What do you mean I can't bring the cats? They are my pets; I have only had them for a few months."

"Okay, good then you are not that attached to them yet so it shouldn't be a problem giving them up," he said firmly.

"I, um, didn't plan on giving them up," I stated.

"Well, it's either me or the cats," he said firmly.

"Ok, well I can't give them up. I mean they are my cats. I would have to give them to someone I know and I don't know anyone who wants three cats," I tried to excuse myself out of this one.

"Well, that's not a problem. My friend Jose lives with his girlfriend Penny. They live on welfare in a big crack house with sixteen cats. I am sure they would be more than happy to take your three cats," Parker said with certainty.

I truly did not feel good about this scenario anymore. I wondered if I should just stay at my grandmother's, yet I had already spoken to her and she had found another tenant.

Therefore, I felt like I had no choice but to give up my cats and move in with Parker.

On a Monday evening, Parker gave me directions to Penny and Jose's crack house. It was a small, two-story contemporary house with wood paneling and worn out unpainted shutters. I opened the torn screen door and knocked on the worn out front door. A petite pretty Hispanic girl with long black hair answered the door. She was maybe eighteen years old.

"Hi," she said with a smile. "Come on in, you must be Jinni. I am Penny.

Jose is just out back, but he should be coming inside soon. Parker told us about you and the three cats. Did you bring them? We will be more than happy to take them for you."

I stepped inside the house smiling as I listened to Penny. I wondered what her life story entailed. She seemed like a very sweet girl. Yet, I wondered why she lived in a crack house and how she got where she was or appeared to be.

I entered the house and stood in what I can only guess was the family room. The room was dimly lighted because the blinds on the windows were drawn up only half way. The floors were carpeted with a matted tan rug. There were cats running everywhere and the stench of cat urine filled the air. Across from the doorway I could see the entrance to the kitchen and to the left of that was a hallway that I imagined went to the bathroom and the bedrooms.

I stood in the entrance faking a smile, ignoring everything I saw and smelled. Then, from out of the kitchen, a little boy about one year old came crawling out. He had very thick black hair and was wearing nothing but a diaper.

"J.J., where are going you silly boy? Where is your Papa?" Penny said in a friendly, loving tone. Then I heard the toilet flush from somewhere down the hallway.

Within seconds, a young, thin, light colored black man of medium height walked in my direction.

"Hi, you must be Jinni. I am José," he said in a very welcoming and friendly manner. I smiled and stretched my hand out to shake his hand. He leaned forward and shook my hand in greeting.

"So I hear you have three cats for us. Bring them anytime, and you can come and visit them any time too," Jose said with a smile. Penny smiled and repeated in echo, "Yes, bring them anytime and you can come and visit them anytime too."

I smiled and looked at Penny, Jose standing in front of me and JJ who was now sitting on the rug in the middle of the living room playing with the cats and kittens that were running around. I did not feel comfortable about any of this, yet like I had done so many times in the past, I ignored my true feelings. I

THE CAT CRACK HOUSE

thought the house was a wreck and I truly did not want to give up my cats. I felt I had no control over my own life or decisions that were made. I seemed to let everyone else make decisions for me.

"Ok, I will bring them by on Saturday morning. Will you be home?" I asked.

"Yes, we will be home. I don't work; although, Jose sometimes works, but usually we are home," Penny humbly said.

"Ok, I will see you around ten in the morning on Saturday then. Thank you," I said.

As I walked to my car, I looked around and realized I was in an obviously run-down drug infested neighborhood, hence the 'crack house'.

By the time Saturday came, I awoke with a knot in my stomach. I really did not want to give away my cats. Despite how I felt, I put the cats in the car and drove them over to the crack house. I got out of the car, leaving the cats where they were and opened the torn screen door. Penny answered the door wearing a long, powder blue pajama pants and a white tank top.

"Hi," I said with a smile. "Sorry if I woke you up," I said feeling guilty. "I um, have my cats in my car. I need some help bringing them in" I continued.

"Sure. Ok, I will help you" Penny sweetly replied. She followed me to my car where she grabbed Pluto. I grabbed Mickey and we quickly brought them inside her house. Then I went back to the car and grabbed Mini. I brought Mini in the house and all three cats just sat there and looked around for a moment before they cautiously began to scatter in fear.

Of all three cats, Mickey was my favorite, but it was very hard for me to leave any of them. I stayed for a few minutes and then searched for each one and gave them each a hug and whispered in their ears, "I am sorry, but you are going to be ok here."

I held my tears back as I thanked Penny and told her that I would like to come back and visit next week. She smiled and assured me that they would be fine and looked forward to my next week's visit.

I walked out to my car, got in and closed the door. I sat there with the key in my hand as I stared at this beat up old crack house and cried.

"What am I doing?" I asked myself. I shook my head in disbelief as tears streamed down my face. I drove home with my heart aching for my three cats.

A week later, before I moved my belongings into Parker's house, I went to visit Mickey, Mini and Pluto. Penny told me that Mini was pregnant. I hadn't even known. I was happy for Mini and when she had the kittens, Penny got in touch with me and I immediately went to visit Mini and her kittens. Mickey and

Pluto were nowhere in sight, and Mini didn't even seem to recognize me. I really felt like I abandoned them.

I wondered what she would say to me if she could talk. I wondered what Pluto and Mickey would say if they could talk too. I suppose it sounds a little funny to wonder what cats would say if they spoke in human language. Who knows? Nevertheless, I could see that Penny was taking care of Mini and I assumed that Mickey and Pluto were just as happy considering they did not even come out from hiding to visit with me.

Parker came over around noon that Saturday and helped me move my stuff into his house. We rented a UHAUL truck for the day. Parker had his brother Randy help with the move. Randy was a bit different than Parker. Parker was a stocky, overweight guy with thick dark hair, blue eyes and a handsome face. His brother was slim and fit, with dark hair and eyes, and was very good looking.

Randy's girlfriend, Hannah also came along to help. Hannah was from Florida where her parents owned a hotel on Hutchinson Island. She was a preppy girl with blonde hair and blue eyes. I liked her; she seemed to be fun.

By five o'clock, we had moved everything into Parker's place. My last visit to my apartment on this day included visiting my grandmother and giving her a big hug.

"I'm a gonna miss a you," my grandmother said in her very thick Italian accent.

"I am going to miss you too grandma, but I will come and visit you,"

I said feeling sad for leaving her.

Parker's house was nice. It was of new construction with one bedroom, one bath, no garage but a full basement. The house was a yellow paneled siding home with black shutters. From the outside it looked like a two-story home, yet when you walked inside, you could see that it was only one floor with cathedral ceilings.

Upon entering was the living room, an open kitchen and dining area. To the far right was the bathroom and on the right was the medium sized bedroom.

That night after moving in, we were watching a movie on television. I sat on the couch and Parker sat in his lazy boy chair. Suddenly, the front door flew open and there stood a petite girl about my age wearing short shorts and a gray shirt baring her right shoulder.

She had short, black, frizzy hair and striking green eyes. She stood in the door way for a moment and stared at me.

"Who's this?" she said in an angry tone.

"This is my new girlfriend," Parker said evenly.

"Oh!" she said, as she turned and slammed the door. "I'll be back for my stuff," I heard her say from outside.

My stomach was knotted on the inside.

"Who was that?" I asked innocently.

"Well, I didn't tell you about her" Parker confessed.

"She's my girlfriend, I mean my ex-girlfriend. We broke up right before you and I got together a month ago. She is still trying to get us back together, but now you are here so she can't come back."

I did not feel very good about this. Was I being used as the new girl friend to make the first girlfriend feel jealous? It certainly seemed that way to me. I did not say this but I certainly thought so.

"Maybe I should move back to my grandmother's" I stated not sure how to respond.

"No, you are not going anywhere. I love you and I don't want you to leave."

I smiled and said, "Okay."

Parker and I had been living together for a few months before I realized his true nature. He was a replica of my ex-boyfriend. Three months of living with someone addicted to smoking pot and drinking was short lived.

Parker was the sort of guy who robbed Peter to pay Paul. He bartered and manipulated his way into every money-making opportunity. Let's just say he wasn't an honest sober or straight sort of chap.

This became very apparent to me when he helped me get my sixteen foot, out-board boat from Jeremy's house. This boat had been my twenty first birthday gift to me from me. I had left it at Jeremy's house because I could not take it with me to my grandmother's house. The motor on the boat had just been repaired when I left Jeremy so I had never had the chance to use the boat. With Parker's help, I got my boat and trailer back. As we moved it from Jeremy's property to Parker's property, little did I imagine what would happen next.

Parker never smiled. In fact all of his teeth were not only nicotine stained, but were rotten at the gum line, so smiling did not help his looks any. Parker had approached me out of the blue and told me that his mouth was in a lot of pain and he needed to go to the dentist. When he returned from the dentist, he was very sweet and sincere as he asked to borrow three thousand dollars in order to have his mouth reconstructed. I told him that I thought that was a lot of money to ask of me and he told me that he would pay me back and promised he would even sign a written document stating that he would pay me back.

I said ok and he did in fact write a promissory note stating that if he did not pay me back, the collateral would be his twenty-one foot Chris-craft house boat and trailer. I thought this was a very good bargain so I gave him the money. A week later, a fire outside awoke us in the middle of the night. Someone had set his boat on fire. Hmmm, I wondered who?

When I went to work the next day, everyone knew about Parker's boat being set on fire. One of our bosses, Glen, said in front of six others, "well, Parker, what do you have for collateral in lieu of return payment to me." Glen intensely.

When Glen walked back to his office I followed him and asked innocently, "Glen, why did you say collateral? What's that all about?"

"Oh! Well, your boyfriend knows how to borrow money but he doesn't know how to pay it back! He hand wrote and signed this collateral note saying that his boat would be used as collateral in lieu of return payment to me." Glen said intently.

I asked Glen to show me the letter that Parker had written him. I took one look at it and said, "I will be right back."

I went to my desk, grabbed my purse and found the folded up promissory letter that Parker had written and signed for me. I went back to Glen's office and asked him to look at my letter. He placed both letters beside each other and we could see that they were identical.

"Humph! Yeah he probably hired someone to burn the boat so he could collect on the insurance money. Jinni, he has no intention of paying either one of us back." Glen said with certainty. I stood there shaking my head in disbelief.

That night Glen came over with his girlfriend. They both sat at the kitchen table. Parker served them beer as Glen stuck his hand in his pocket and pulled out a small pouch of white powder. He poured it on the glass kitchen table and began to form rows of cocaine to snort. I was shocked! I could not believe my eyes.

"So, Parker, how much ya think you're gonna get for the boat?" Glen said as he stood up after snorting his first line.

"Glen I told ya, I don't know, probably nothing. My insurance expired because I hadn't been keeping up with the payments," Parker said in defense.

"Yeah, sure Parker..... am I supposed to believe that? Come and do a line." Glen said.

"Hey, Jinni come on, you ever try cocaine?" Glen said but didn't look at me.

"Um......no. I never tried cocaine," I said. What I really wanted to say was that I never wanted to try it, but I didn't say that. I shut down my inner feelings because I was frightened. There was my boss, his girlfriend and my boyfriend hanging out snorting cocaine and wanting me to snort some as well.

"Well, come on down and try some, the price is right," Glen said mimicking the talk show host from the old television game show, "The Price is Right".

I walked over to the table and faked a smile. I sat down and I did a line right in front of my boss. I was definitely no pro at this but I tried to look cool and fit in, yet I felt stupid. I had sat at the table as everyone had gotten up and Glen said, "Let's all go out somewhere."

Parker immediately said, "Hey let's just hang out here; I got some really good weed we can smoke."

"Ha ha ha. Now you're talking my man! I like your style. Ok, we're staying here!" Glen said as he made himself comfortable in the television room.

I sat there observing the present moments and felt my life was truly warped. As I was stuck in my head in thought, I contemplated moving out of state to be closer to one of my parents. I had known that my boyfriend of now 4 months had his mother living in Florida, as did my Mother. Regardless of my reality and how I truly wanted to break free from living with this guy, we moved together to Florida in August 2010.

After being in Florida for one week, I had an unsettled feeling in my stomach about living with Parker. Yet, as always I ignored my true feelings and went along with Parker as if I had no say in the matter. Some way, somehow, I found my strength and I told Parker that I did not want to continue to be in a relationship with him and that I was going to get my own place just as soon as I was able to get my stuff off the moving truck when it arrived.

Knowing the moving truck would be arriving a week after we did, I requested and paid for the moving truck to make there first stop at my mother's house. My mother had her own life story going on. She had been renting out a room from her first cousin Howard, a very successful paralegal that lived very comfortably in a seven bedroom house. This is where I had planned to keep my stuff and live temporarily.

Parker was there to witness the truck unloading my stuff and he freaked out and yelled, "WAIT! I need to get on that truck and make sure you don't take my stuff!"

The drivers, as well as my mother and I, looked at each other with a puzzled look on our faces. Parker went on to the truck and within five minutes walked off the truck with a five pound bag of marijuana. The rest of us all looked at each other with our mouths wide open in shock. The drivers told Parker that if they had gotten pulled over and had their truck inspected, they would have lost their jobs because of Parker's choice to have drugs moved on this delivery from New York to Florida.

My mother got to see first-hand how manipulative and corrupt Parker truly was. I never heard my mother curse at anyone as much as she cursed at Parker. Not only did she curse at him, she made sure to tell him what a loser she thought he was. I moved in with my Mother and completely disconnected myself from Parker and began a new life for myself: A new life, a new state, a new everything.

That's my story up to now, Ms. Lisa. I have been afraid to contact you at times, yet I have reached out to you from time to time as you already know. I feel really lucky to know you. You have been a friend and you have consistently been a support for me, even though I have kept my distance over the years. You have been an inspiration to me and although, my life has been on a really rough road, your love and support have kept me reaching for a better life. Maybe that is what God is to some people, he is always there and hopes that we will make better choices because we can have a better life if we want that.

Thank you for caring.
Wish me luck!
~Love Jinni

THE THREE OF LIFE
reminds me to think about:

1. **ATTITUDE** = Walking next to the ocean there are hundreds of sea shells that wash up on shore. I could pick up every seashell that I have attracted in my walk, or I can choose the ones I want and leave the rest. This also goes true for the people we attract in our lives. Yet, it becomes unhealthy when we find ourselves picking up everyone that washes up on our shore. This is when we need to be aware of the choices we make in allowing others in our inner circle of life.

2. **LOVE** = Possibly in everyone's life, there are specific Angels that are assigned to be in our life to teach us the greatest lessons. When we think about those difficult people in our lives, I must ask myself," What would love do?"

3. **HEALTHY RELATIONSHIPS** = Pets are a healthy extension of our family circle. When we are faced with having to make a choice in giving up our pets in order to comply with another persons wish, we are not honoring the relationship we have originally created for ourselves.

"*Scoundrels are always sociable.*"
~ Arthur Schopenhauer, 1788-1862

Attitude, Love and The Pursuit of Healthy Relationships

Dear Jinni-

I must be the only one left in the world that still mails out, Dear letters…..lol. We have spoken a few times on the telephone over the past couple of years. I am here to support you in all that you do. So many times there is so much I want to say to you, yet, I know better to listen.

I felt that in writing you this letter, I could better express myself. Possibly you will hold on to this letter and re-read it from time to time.

I believe in you and I know that the cards of life that you have played have not been simple cards. They say in life that we pre-determine our life before we are even here and I believe this to be true. Your greatest challenges have been your greatest teachers.

I am so proud of you that you have re-connected with your Mother. I wish you only the best that life offers. Always keep in mind that you are the creator of your own universe. Do not reflect your future on your past, instead, learn from it.

You are more than you know and only you can plant the seeds that will bloom tomorrow. Only you are in control of you. I am always here to support you, regardless of where you are in life. Always remember who you are and take care of yourself first.

You know to well, that when we 'jump' at opportunities or even new relationships, they never seem to work out. If it helps, think about that homemade sauce you ate with pasta when you came to visit me at my home. That sauce you loved so much, was not made in five or even ten minutes. That sauce had been simmering for at least eight hours. The point I am making is that, anything that is great, takes time to simmer before its ready.

As you continue in your walk of life keep in mind, your *Attitude*, your *Love* and the importance of *Healthy Relationships*. In everything you do remember to stop and give yourself breathing space before beginning a new venture, whether it be a new job or a new partnership/relationship. Here are some tips to help you in your journey of life;

1. ~ATTITUDE~ Attitude is EVERYTHING!!!
2. ~LOVE~ We each need love to survive. Love begins for each one of us, within ourselves first. If you want to have a loving

relationship, love yourself first. Be forgiving of what and who you are not. Love yourself for all that you are. You are tailored to be just perfect the way you are.
3. ~RELATIONSHIPS~

Everywhere you go and everything you do, involves people. Your attitude is everything. Love is something we all need to survive and share with others. Relationships are unavoidable! There are relationships within your family, amongst your friends, as well as co-workers.

Networking and keeping your job is not what your attitude is. What your attitude is towards your job and how you relate to co-workers and others is your attitude. It will never matter what you do for work, whether you decide to work for the sanitation department or are a traveling super star, your attitude along with your actions and re-actions will speak volumes for who you are.

My dad used to manage a company, Pan American Airlines. Maybe you have heard of it, maybe not. Never the less, my dad used to say stuff like, "I am the meanest son of a -, but I know how to get the job done right and people respect me!" And he was right! People did respect him because they were so very intimidated by him. They were afraid they would loose their jobs if they did or said anything out of line. I don't know if that is good housekeeping, per say. But I can tell you that at his funeral, friends of my dads were there that had known him for twenty and thirty years. I cannot say that I would follow my dads attitude, but I can say my dad did leave a legacy of dedication and commitment to do what's right and honorable. My dad's attitude is how people saw him. Yet you could see that his exterior was only so thick as he deeply loved his work and his family. Why am I telling you all of this Jinni? I suppose I cannot express myself more when I say that relationships last forever if you want them to. And as we move on in life, as we all do, what you have left behind is a piece of your attitude to be remembered by. It is said that throughout our lifetimes, we touch and impact at least ten thousand others whom we have come in contact with. The funny truth about this is that you never know whose lives you are impacting. Whenever you are in a doubtful situation step back and re-evaluate the circumstances, your re-actions speak your truth. Ask yourself what love would do, in any given situation.

Always remember, that you are never alone. You are always in a relationship with others. So, every now and again don't be afraid to do a reality check on your attitude, your love for yourself and the relationships you have.

Think about what you really want, and honor yourself. Spend time with you and you shall see how special you are. I have always believed that it is so easy to get lost in someone else when we have never taken the time claim ourselves first. Each one of us is perfectly willing to learn from unpleasant experience—if only the damage of the first lesson could be repaired. Allow time to do its job, let time heal—with time.

My greatest wish for you Jinni; Is that you find your THREE OF LIFE and live by it. Experiences change lives and attitudes. Give yourself permission to make bigger and better changes in your life. May you be at peace with yourself and with the choices you make in your life. If you are not happy, then make needed changes. If that is not possible, ask yourself why not?

Jinni, always remember that whether or not you believe in God know that he does believe in you. Believe in yourself! Everything begins with you. Know that you are loved and that you are special. Give yourself space to grow and be all that you have been created to be. Listen to that inner voice, it is your God given guide to your universe. Embrace that voice and trust it. When you follow that inner voice and not the outer, you will see how everything in your life transforms to what you have aligned yourself with, from your inner guidance.

Hardships and tough times are always temporary. Being 'stuck' is not an option ;)

SMILE, and stay safe and BE HAPPY! (It always beats the alternative!)

In closing of this letter, t is time to give yourself permission to enter the doorway of loving, inspirational, abundance, prosperity and ultimate possibilities!

Always expect the best when you open a door............

I love you Jinni- Be well, and keep in touch!
Your mentor and forever friend,
with much love~
Ms. Lisa

"Our attitude towards what has happened to us in life is the important thing to recognize. Once hopeless, my life is now hope-full, but it did not happen overnight. The last of human freedoms, to choose one's attitude in any given set of circumstances, is to choose one's own way."

-Victor Frankl

EPILOGUE

I truly believe it is possible to live several lives in the existing body in which we are contained. It is all a matter of the mind-set we keep and what we change about ourselves. It is not so much that the world changes around us, but more so, that our view of life changes. Our attitude, our love for self and the pursuit of healthy relationships change.

Since I have written this book, what I have realized through Jinni's story is that;

One of the greatest choices we have in life is to choose our friends. They say we are whom we associate with. Influence is the creator of our tomorrow. So, why not surround yourself with positive, inspirational people. Because all we truly want in life is to be happy today and to look forward to an even better tomorrow.

I am so very thankful for all the mentors and teachers that have touched my life in inspiring ways. I am also grateful for my family and friends. Without their support I don't know if I would be where I am today. It is with great honor and joy for me to give back and be a mentor and support others in their walk of life.

There are no mistakes in life just lessons to learn from our weakest moments. Take a step back from life in order to rearrange and prioritize. This is what has worked for me. Maybe these tools will work for you too. With a will to survive, my mind continues to grow stronger and wiser and realize that life does not need to be so challenging and difficult. I realize that we are all 100% in control of ourselves and the decisions we make.

THE THREE OF LIFE
reminds me to think about:

1. **ATTITUDE** = I have learned first-hand that healthy relationships are the key to good health and well-being, both mentally and physically.

2. **LOVE** = The greatest relationship you will ever have is the one you have with yourself. You are number one!

3. **HEALTHY RELATIONSHIPS** = There are few choices in this life we live. Dr. Wayne Dwyer once said, "Friends are God's apology for your family members." So, CHOOSE your friends wisely. Choose the ones that inspire and uplift you.

"*Resolve to be thyself; and know that he, who finds himself, loses his Misery.*"

~MATTHEW ARNOLD, 1822-1888

"There are two ways of spreading light: to be the candle, or the mirror that reflects it."

~Edith Wharton 1862-1912

Lisa Eva Gold is the Author of "A Will to Survive ". Lisa is a dedicated, certified Visionary Life and Health Coach and Speaker, with the John Maxwell Group.

Lisa is also a graduate of BRIFT, (Burt Reynolds Institute For Theater—2007/2010). She spent four years attending Master Acting classes taught by Burt Reynolds.

Lisa claims herself to be a tree with many branches. She dedicates her time and attention towards always re- creating herself as a Teacher, an Actor, Director, Producer, Musician, Mentor, Author and Writer. You can see Lisa on television shows like Burn Notice as well as various commercials, and occasional theater productions. She also continues to work on independent films.

Lisa is a Christian that is especially dedicated to mentoring foster children and is an activist in bringing awareness to the community in regard to stopping domestic violence and human trafficking.

You can personally contact Lisa for coaching and mentoring at justplaypiano@yahoo.com

Look for my next book "I am But A Quilt", available in the fall of 2012.

Recommended Readings:

"Letting Go of the Person You Used to Be" by Lama Surya Das

"The 7 Wonders That Will Change Your Life" By John Beck

"The Most Brilliant Thoughts of All Time" Edited by John M. Shanahan

"The Road Not Taken" A Selection of Robert Frost's Poems with an Introduction and Commentary by Louis Untermeyer

"Modern Drama, Poetry, and Essays" Singer/Random House literature series

"Born For Love/Reflections on Loving" By Leo Buscaglia

"Beyond Positive Thinking" By Jim Collins

"Boundaries" By Dr. Henry Cloud & Dr. John Townsend

"The Celestine Prophecy" By James Redfield

"Awakening Intuition" By Mona Lisa Schulz

"Combing The Mirror" By Rev. Keving Ross Emery

"The Map" By Colette Baron-Reid

"Teach Me How To Love" By Scott Kalechestein Grace

"The 21 Irrefutable Laws of Leadership" By John C Maxwell

"Leadership GOLD" By John C Maxwell

"Forgive to Win!" Walter E. Jacobson M.D.

"The Holy Bible" Inspired through God

Recommended CDs':

DISSOLVING BARRIERS By Louise L. Hay
OVERCOMING FEARS/CREATING SAFETY FOR YOU AND YOUR WORLD By Louise L. Hay
FORGIVNESS/LOVING THE INNER CHILD By Louise L. Hay

Recommended Web-Sites:

www.justplayproductions.org
www.Wikipedia.org

Recommended Viewing:

"The Shift" DVD, by Dr. Wayne Dyer
"By making better choices today, you can count on great tomorrows."

THE THREE OF LIFE

Attitude, Love and the Pursuit of Healthy Relationships
http://www.thethreeoflifebook.yolasite.com/

www.ingramcontent.com/pod-product-compliance
Lightning Source LLC
Chambersburg PA
CBHW062223080426
42734CB00010B/2003